Interactive Open Educational Resources

A GUIDE TO FINDING, CHOOSING, AND USING WHAT'S OUT THERE TO TRANSFORM COLLEGE TEACHING

John D. Shank

JB JOSSEY-BASS™
A Wiley Brand

ACRL
Advancing learning
Transforming scholarship
Association of College & Research Libraries
A division of the American Library Association

Published by Jossey-Bass
A Wiley Brand
One Montgomery Street, Suite 1200, San Francisco, CA 94104-4594-www.josseybass.com

Jossey-Bass books and products are available through most bookstores. To contact Jossey-Bass directly call our Customer Care Department within the U.S. at 800-956-7739, outside the U.S. at 317-572-3986, or fax 317-572-4002.

Wiley publishes in a variety of print and electronic formats and by print-on-demand. Some material included with standard print versions of this book may not be included in e-books or in print-on-demand. If this book refers to media such as a CD or DVD that is not included in the version you purchased, you may download this material at http://booksupport.wiley.com. For more information about Wiley products, visit www.wiley.com.

Library of Congress Cataloging-in-Publication Data
Library of Congress Cataloging-in-Publication Data has been applied for and is on file with the Library of Congress.
ISBN 978-1-118-27745-4 (paper); ISBN 978-1-118-41967-0 (ebk.); ISBN 978-1-118-42156-7 (ebk.)

Printed in the United States of America

FIRST EDITION
PB Printing 10 9 8 7 6 5 4 3 2 1

The Jossey-Bass Higher and
Adult Education Series

CONTENTS

Preface: Transforming the Learning Experience through New Forms of
    Instructional Materials in the Digital Information Age   ix
About the Author   xv

PART ONE Interactive Learning Materials: Setting the Stage   1

ONE Interactive Learning Materials: Engaging Learners in the
Emerging Digital World   3

TWO Defining an Emergent Class of Educational Resources:
Interactive Multimedia Modules, Simulations, and Games   11

PART TWO Finding ILMs: A Digital Exploration   19

THREE The Discovery Process: The Art of Discovering ILMs   21

FOUR The Pioneers: Searching Online Educational Repositories
in North America and the United Kingdom   35

FIVE The Educators: Searching College and University
Educational Repositories   61

SIX The Entrepreneurs: Textbook Publishers, Entertainment
Media, and Educational Software Companies   83

SEVEN The Exhibitors: Museums, Professional Organizations,
and Governmental Organizations   95

PART THREE Choosing and Using ILMs   111

EIGHT The Selection Process: How to Choose and Evaluate
ILMs   113

NINE The Implementation Process: How to Instruct and
Engage Students through ILMs   129

TEN The Assessment Process: The Impact of ILMs on Student
Learning   143

Epilogue: How Faculty, Librarians, and Instructional Support Staff
    Transform Learning with ILMs in the Future   155

References   163

Index   169

To my family, who explore life to the fullest with me:

Jennifer, Katie, Sam, Daniel, Sarah, Rebecca, and Rachel

To my mentors and friends who inspire me:

C. Patrick Kohrman, Robert Erb, Diane Lovelace, Deena Morganti,
Gregory Crawford, and Steven Bell

To my colleagues who helped make this particular work possible:

Marjory Kruppenbach, Mary Ann Mengel, Amy Roche, Tricia Clark,
and Nancy Dewald

Transforming the Learning Experience through New Forms of Instructional Materials in the Digital Information Age

MOVING FROM DISRUPTIVE INNOVATION TO CONSTRUCTIVE INNOVATION

Higher education is under tremendous pressure to change. This change is being driven by technological, economic, and political pressures that are unlikely to lessen anytime soon. Such pressures are disruptive and force universities and colleges to reexamine how they operate. Whether it is changing the cost structure to make higher education more affordable; improving students' success, retention, and graduation; or the government divesting itself of supporting public state schools, change is on the horizon. The nature, extent, and impact of those changes are uncertain, but what is certain is that disruptive change tends to be chaotic, traumatic, and at times destructive. These vicissitudes lead to an environment where problems and complications must then be fixed for an organization to survive and thrive.

Is there another path? One that is more constructive than destructive even in the face of ever increasing technological, economic, and political pressures? What if higher education could innovate, not disruptively but in an ordered and systematic way? Could there be certain paths to change that will not utterly break or destroy systems and structures but rather will evolve them by complementing and enhancing? This kind of change is more beneficial and successive, transforming an existing system constructively instead of destructively. In higher education, where the focus has shifted from the faculty teaching to the students learning, tremendous opportunities await us. Contemporary, digital computing technologies now afford us the prospect of transforming our institutions either disruptively or constructively. The choice is ours unless we refuse to act.

One such constructive opportunity for change in the teaching and learning environment and in libraries of higher education lays just on the horizon. This is the broad adoption of a new set of open, online, interactive, educational resources. These digital resources are plentiful and largely free. They are interactive, multimedia educational materials such as learning modules (i.e., tutorials with practice exercises), educational games, and simulations — interactive learning materials (ILMs).

ENVISIONING INSTRUCTIONAL TRANSFORMATION IN HIGHER EDUCATION

The future is a difficult thing to predict. This is eloquently reflected in Paul Valery's famous quote, "The trouble with our times is that the future is not what it used to be." How we imagine the future changes with time and context. Looking back at how the past envisions the future we find that it can almost accurately predict some elements of a future reality. For example, the 1967 film *1999 A.D.* predicted that students would be learning from the comfort of their homes, submissively receiving audiovisual lessons on a giant almost colorless flat-screen television and then being tested using a teaching machine (Novack, 1967).

While thankfully this vision of the future has not completely come true, some of its elements exist today. The Internet and home computers do allow students to watch multimedia content at home, and learning management systems (e.g., Blackboard) make it easy to test students on course and lesson content. Unlike the aforementioned picture, today's students are not relegated merely to being passive receptacles, simply sitting in front of screens watching a lesson. Rather, games, simulations, and interactive multimedia educational modules (i.e., tutorials with practice exercises) exist to more fully engage the learner. This engagement is critical for those of the Screenagers/Net generation because it necessitates that they take an active role in their learning. It also provides them with an appealing and enhanced learning environment that offers guidance and feedback.

These types of resources are increasingly being created by textbook publishers, educational broadcast entertainment media, educational software publishers, professional and governmental organizations, museums, and institutions of higher education. This trend is not likely to abate. It is more likely to accelerate in the near future as a result of technological and societal trends that move us toward creating more gratifying, immersive learning environments at home and in the classroom. Soon, students will have access to high-definition, three-dimensional, multiuser virtual learning environments with motion sensors and voice recognition. Combining these technologies with the development of mobile devices that operate as both a cell phone and tablet PC allowing students to access the Internet with screens large enough to make it easy to read and view class materials will enable learners to collect, store, and access class materials easily, conveniently, anytime and anywhere.

All of these innovations, along with the creation of online digital libraries and repositories that share open educational resources (OERs), point to a future in which traditional print resources such as textbooks, books, and magazines are no longer the only or perhaps even the primary resource educators will use to teach their students. Rather, in a universe of digital materials these traditionally passive resources will share only a piece of the pie with more interactive and visually satisfying course content.

One of the critical challenges of our time is successfully transforming the current centuries-old print-based system that finds, collects, organizes, and provides access to learning materials (i.e., the library with its books, journals, and newspapers). Libraries were constructed in a predigital age. To remain relevant, we must rethink, reenvision, and ultimately transform how libraries perform the same functions that they have been responsible for in the past. This task must take place in a world populated by digital natives who want instant access to all types of online, digital materials that afford them the opportunity to be immersed within the chosen resource as well as to connect with others using it (Prensky, 2010).

MOVING TO A NEW PARADIGM WITH INTERACTIVE LEARNING MATERIALS

A critical challenge for all educators today is to be able to effectively and efficiently locate and integrate these new types of interactive educational resources into their curricula, courses, and libraries. This guidebook offers a practical primer on ILMs. It intends to help inform and guide faculty, librarians, educational technologists, instructional designers, administrators, and interested students in successfully finding, choosing, and using ILMs. In so doing, the goal of this work will be achieved—that is, providing access to the vast and quickly expanding universe of digital learning materials available on the Internet (either freely in OERs or for a fee through publishers) by enabling educators to quickly locate and effectively integrate these resources into their face-to-face, online, or blended/hybrid courses.

This book will first examine why and how ILMs can enhance student learning. Research has shown that several critical factors (i.e., time on task, learning style, and instructor feedback) can affect and potentially enhance student learning (U.S. Department of Education, 2010). Interactive learning materials have the ability to enhance the student learning experience and to engage learners with activities that can challenge, stimulate, and enrich their minds and thus can lead to increased time on task and improved learning (Barr and Tagg, 1995). Most ILMs include multiple communication modalities so that they can facilitate learning in students with different learning styles. Finally, assessment and feedback are critical in helping both the instructor and student evaluate the learner's understanding of the material. High-quality, well-designed ILMs provide feedback to students as they progress through the content and often integrate some form of assessment to determine the level of mastery they have achieved over the content as a result of using the resource.

Chapter 2 explores what ILMs are and what they are not. Interactive learning materials are a type (or subset) of OERs that can fit within the definition of a *learning object*. However, ILMs are more expressly thought of as any digital, interactive, and multimedia resource containing a specific set of learning objectives used for an instructional purpose. The three distinct types of ILMs are (1) learning modules (i.e., interactive, multimedia tutorials with practice exercises); (2) educational simulations; and (3) educational games. The three critical components of a well-designed ILM are (1) interactivity that engages learners and requires them to actively participate in comprehending the content; (2) several modalities used in presenting the content (e.g., audio, visual, kinesthetic); and (3) assessment components that test and inform learners about their understanding of the material. Chapter 2 also provides general criteria for how all educators, whether faculty, staff, or administrators, can evaluate and select the highest quality ILMs for their students.

The subsequent chapters (Chapters 3–7) discuss in detail the discovery process for finding and transferring these types of resources into the instructor's curriculum. The book will examine some of the best repositories, referatories, and digital library websites available from educational organizations, colleges and universities, textbook and educational entertainment publishers and media, and museums, professional organizations, and governmental organizations to find high-quality ILMs. Additionally, these chapters explore the best practices and techniques for successfully searching these sites. To make this work as relevant and practical as possible, short video tutorials (sorry, no practice exercises included) will be linked and continually updated.

The final chapters of the book briefly examine some of the best methods for integrating ILMs into instructors' course assignments and for assessing their impact on student learning. Chapter 9 reviews the benefits of integrating ILMs into institutions' learning management systems (e.g., Blackboard, Desire2Learn, Moodle, Sakai), such as allowing instructors to assess and track students' use of the resources. The tracking features gives instructors the ability to see how much time students are spending engaged with course materials and how well they are performing and understanding the content. Chapter 10 focuses on some of the most effective methods educators can employ to demonstrate ILMs' impact on student learning. The Epilogue explores how partnerships and teams of faculty, librarians, and instructional support staff (i.e., instructional designers and technologists) can work together to enhance student learning by integrating high-quality ILMs into the curriculum.

Imagine a world where students are excited to use course resources and where they spend more time engaged with their course work. Imagine educators being able to better know what each of their students has mastered and what they still struggle with. Or envision instructors being able to assign ILMs that can remediate student learning gaps through automated activities (i.e., online games, simulations, and tutorials) to be completed outside of class anywhere students have access to the Web.

This is just a glimpse of the potential of ILMs. Their benefits far exceed their costs. By using existing high-quality ILMs, partnerships between faculty, librarians, information technologists, educational technologists, instructional designers, and other interested staff and administrators can potentially enhance student performance, retention, and satisfaction. The only cost to faculty is the time that it takes to locate and integrate these resources into their courses—granted, this is not a simple and easy process yet. That is where this book comes in. It will benefit anyone who desires to practice the most effective and efficient methods of finding, choosing, and using ILMs. And it will enable all educators and students to employ these highly interactive digital resources to enhance the educational learning environment in their courses and, once widely adopted, ultimately to transform student learning in higher education.

HOW TO USE THIS VOLUME

This book is meant to be a practical guidebook for any instructor, librarian, or educational technologist desiring to learn more about ILMs and how to locate, select, and use them. To this end, the book is organized to help orient faculty who are not familiar with these resources by providing an overview of ILMs. Additionally, the synopses are designed to provide a quick overview of the most significant themes in the chapters. The book includes a basic and advanced searching section that can yield better results. The Going Further section provides a primer of significant resources that can help readers explore more in-depth the germane topics. The index can also function as a quick means of navigating the entire work.

This work is also intended for librarians, who can support faculty in the process of finding high-quality ILMs, as well as instructional designers, developers, and technologists, who can assist faculty with integrating and utilizing the educational resources. Consequently, this book is separated into three distinct sections. While the book is intended to be used in its entirety, it can be employed for simply identifying good resources to use in locating appropriate interactive learning materials and recognizing the best techniques to search those sources. Because of the nature of Web resources and their ability to quickly be updated and revised, integrated links are included in sections that review the digital libraries, databases, and repositories and will routinely be updated with videos showing the best practices and techniques for searching each of the sources contained in this book. Additionally, a quick search guide (Table 4.1) is included at the beginning of Chapter 4 to make it easier for readers to very swiftly determine the best starting source to find ILMs related to the topic or discipline for which they are looking.

ABOUT THE AUTHOR

John D. Shank received his master's degree from Drexel University and his baccalaureate degree from Earlham College. The strengths of these institutions in teaching and learning, academic libraries, and information technology shaped his views of the important interconnection that exists between them. Shank has held various positions within the libraries and information technology department at Bryn Mawr College, Haverford College, and Montgomery County Community College, all of which further informed and guided the development of his passion for his vocation.

Currently, Shank is a tenured full librarian faculty member (instructional design librarian) within the Pennsylvania State University Libraries. He is also founding director of the Center for Learning & Teaching at Penn State's Berks College. He has responsibilities across many of the boundaries of higher educational life, including teaching, administration, research, and service. He teaches CAS 283 (Communication and Information Technology) and CAS 383 (Culture & Technology). Nearly a decade ago, he developed the Berks Educational Technology Grant Curriculum Program at Penn State and since that time has directed more than ninety large and small grant projects that have been awarded to faculty, initially impacting over one hundred courses and more than 3,500 students. These initiatives have focused on enhancing the student-centered teaching and learning environment.

His research interests include the role, use, and impact of instructional technologies in higher education and academic libraries. In this capacity, Shank has been an invited consultant and speaker; has been interviewed by the *Christian Science Monitor*, the *Chronicle of Higher Education*, and *American Libraries*;

and has given hundreds of presentations at conferences, meetings, webinars, and workshops. Moreover, Shank has authored and coauthored a book, book chapters, research studies, and articles that focus on library integration into learning management systems, digital learning materials (learning objects), and the development of instructional design librarian positions.

Over the past decade, he has both served on committees and been a member of numerous professional organizations including the Association of College and Research Libraries, Library and Information Technology Association, Teaching and Learning with Technology Group, IMS Global Learning Consortium, Multimedia Educational Resource for Learning and Online Teaching (MERLOT), EDUCAUSE's Learning Objects Virtual Community of Practice, and editorial boards for *Internet Reference Services Quarterly* and reviewer for *College & Research Libraries* and *Pennsylvania Libraries: Research & Practice*. Shank has also served on or chaired dozens of committees at Penn State. Along with Steven Bell, he is the cofounder and advisory board cochair of the Blended Librarian On-line Community (http://www.blendedlibrarian.org/). Shank was selected by *Library Journal* in 2005 as a Mover and Shaker for his role in using technology to integrate newly emerging learning resources in higher education.

PART ONE

Interactive Learning Materials: Setting the Stage

Today, computers are common in every classroom from kindergarten to college. Over the past three decades, children have been exposed to technology from a very early age and have grown up playing video games and using computers both at home and school. These digital natives, known formally as the Net Generation, have always lived in a world with computers. Combined with the arrival of the Internet, these technologies have profound implications for current and future students as well as for preceding generations.

These implications are broad ranging and will reshape our society and educational system in the Information Age. Entire industries (i.e., music, entertainment, and publishing) will be impacted by evolving technologies. Where these paradigm shifts intersect this book lies within the changing nature of the type of resources we have used to educate our students. For decades, textbooks, journals, and newspapers (more recently videos) have served as the primary resources for course curricula, but in the near future that paradigm will shift. Because of the Internet and mobile computing technologies, a whole host of newer and developing formats of information will be increasingly accessible to students. The following chapters set the stage for exploring these newer formats and the advantages they offer.

Interactive Learning Materials

Engaging Learners in the Emerging Digital World

We shape our tools and afterwards our tools shape us.

— Marshall McLuhan

Today's students are digital natives; they are a generation of students that like to be constantly connected with content that allows them to watch, listen, read, and (most critically) interact with their technology-rich environment (Prensky, 2001; Oblinger and Oblinger, 2005). Unlike the generation of many of today's instructors, they have never lived in a world that does not let them interact with their entertainment and communication environment. The idea of passively sitting back and gathering around the radio or television to simply watch and listen to a show is becoming increasingly foreign to today's students.

For centuries, instructors have been faced with the challenge of finding ways to motivate, engage, and help students learn critical course content. The difference today is that our students live in a world where they can interact and connect with the shows they watch. For example, *American Idol* allows them to vote by texting a message directly to the show using a cell phone or wireless Internet-enabled device. Likewise, they live in a digital multitasking world that allows them simultaneously to play games, chat over the Internet with friends anywhere, and listen to music. Educators today, most of whom are considered digital immigrants (I am certainly one), compete more fiercely now than ever before for their students' attention. One of their primary challenges is cultivating students' intellectual curiosity and interest.

THE RISE OF INTERACTIVE LEARNING MATERIALS

Computer digital technologies have given rise to the development of all types of resources. This includes the digitization of more traditional resources such as books, magazines, and newspapers as well as the creation of new forms of digital information formats such as podcasts, videos, and animations. The tremendous proliferation of online learning materials has been concurrent with the growth of open educational resources (OERs), which include all types of learning materials that are licensed to be freely available for educational, nonprofit use (Johnstone, 2005; Atkins, Brown, and Hammond, 2007).

A smaller but rapidly expanding subset of educational resources attempts to integrate active learning components digitally into its material (Barkley, 2010) to engage learners with the goal of holding their attention. Called interactive learning materials (ILMs), they—and the various types of digital informational formats they represent (e.g., interactive, multimedia modules that contain tutorials with practice exercises, games, and simulations)—build on more traditionally passive learning materials like text, audio, and video content to create a new format of learning resources that moves beyond requiring students to simply listen or view the course material.

Why are these types of digital educational resources rapidly becoming vital resources for faculty and students to enhance both classroom and online learning? To begin to answer this question we must examine the components of well-designed ILMs. Broadly speaking, three major components need to be incorporated into ILMs to make them more effective than the traditional learning tools: (1) some type of interactivity that engages learners and requires them to actively participate in comprehending the content; (2) combination of several modalities in presenting the content (e.g., audio, visual, kinesthetic); and (3) assessment and feedback component that tests and informs learners about their level of understanding of the material.

It is helpful to examine in detail a well-designed module (i.e., containing a tutorial with practice exercises) that was created using the basic instructional design process ADDIE (Analyze, Design, Develop, Implement, and Evaluate). (Note to faculty: This is a collaboration opportunity with instructional design or technology staff at your institution because they are experts in instructional design models; also see Going Further: Recommended Reading at the end of this chapter to learn more about this topic.) ADDIE was employed to create an ILM that could gain students' attention and assist them in better understanding course content. The tutorials with practice exercises come from a group of introductory calculus modules created by the Center for Learning & Teaching (CLT) at the Berks College of the Pennsylvania State University (Penn State Berks, 2012). The tutorials use Robert Gagne's Nine Events of Instruction as a foundation to create instructional events to facilitate and improve students' learning of calculus (Briggs, Gustafson, and Tillman, 1991). The more aspects the learning modules contain, the more likely it is that the learning modules will enhance student learning:

1. *Gaining the learners attention:* This requires developing a learning environment for the ILM that students find relevant, appealing, and enjoyable to use. A goal of any ILM is to increase learner engagement with the content by having them interact with the content as it is presented and practiced, thereby increasing the "time on task" with the instructor's student learning objectives and course concepts. A benefit to learners is that as they spend more time engaged with the content of the course they will generally perform better in demonstrating course learning objectives (Chickering and Ehrmann, 1996).

2. *Explicitly stating the ILMs' objectives:* What outcomes will students be able to demonstrate if they have learned or mastered the material? The use of specific, measurable learning objectives allows for an accurate assessment of the knowledge and/or skills gained after completing the resource. The benefit to learners is that by having a clear statement presented of what they are expected to learn, they can better understand what they should focus on/pay attention to while using the ILM.

3. *Reminding learners of relevant prior knowledge:* This is necessary to guide learners to remediate any missed or forgotten knowledge so that it can be used as a building block for learning new material. The benefit to learners is that by including essential prior knowledge through instructional scaffolding they will be more likely to understand the new material and successfully move on to learning new content (August, Lopez, Yokomoto, and Buchanan, November 2002).

4. *Stimulating learners:* A critical component of any well-designed ILM, this requires learners to respond to visual, auditory, and tactile stimuli necessitating that they take some action to proceed through the resource. The benefit to learners is that they will be able to identify with one or more of the various media and sensory modalities depending on their preferred learning style, which will enhance their engagement with the tutorial (Gagné, Wager, Golas, and Keller, 2005).

5. *Providing learning guidance:* This correlates to both the ILM design (i.e., it is easy and intuitive to use, like turning the next page in a book) and the process and structure by which learners navigate or are guided step by step, linearly or nonlinearly, using visuals, examples, or case studies to facilitate new knowledge and understanding of the material. The benefit to learners is reduced confusion and ambiguity in navigating the tutorial content, which enhances their ability to process the content (Churchill, 2007).

6. *Eliciting learner performance:* This relates directly to learner stimulation and guidance. ILMs should require learners to practice the skill or demonstrate an understanding of the new knowledge gained through repeated practice exercises that confirm or deny their mastery of the material and also helps them remember it. The benefit to learners is the ability to demonstrate and practice their newly acquired knowledge, which helps to reinforce the learning that has taken place.

7. *Providing learner feedback:* This lets learners know immediately if they correctly understand the resources objectives. Also, the specificity of the feedback can inform learners about existing gaps in their understanding of the material and what actions they may need to take to gain a better understanding. The benefit to learners is that the feedback aids them in knowing they have either correctly or incorrectly applied the concepts or skills to be learned and also reinforces the correct information. Additionally, the corrective feedback guides the learner so that they can have a better idea of why they answered incorrectly and know what step or action they should take to arrive at the correct solution.

8. *Assessing learner performance:* Activities, tests, or quizzes confirm learners' level of understanding as a result of completing the ILM and provide additional coaching, feedback, or hints that can help them be more successful in the future. The benefit to learners is that enhanced learner responses reveal to both the instructor and learner what learning has or has not occurred. The summative assessment can enable the learner to better understand the concepts they grasped and recognize those that they still struggle with understanding.

9. *Enhancing learner retention and transfer to the real world:* The context with which learners frame the ILM is vital to helping them see its relevance and authenticity to the real world. This component of Gagne's Nine Events of Instruction most closely aligns with cognitive constructivism (Schuh and Barab, 2008). A good example of this is demonstrated in the Accounting 211 module (Penn State Berks, 2011) in which students play the role of an accountant for a company called Veggie Deli to demonstrate their mastery of T-accounts and debits and credits. The benefit to learners is that they are better able to understand and apply how the concepts they are learning are relevant and can be applied to their future career goals and workplace expectations.

SYNOPSIS

Current and future generations of students who are growing up in the networked computing and digital information age are oriented toward their surrounding environment in ways researchers still do not understand (Hargittai, 2010; Helsper and Eynon, 2010; Jones et al., 2010). These digital natives were raised with radically different technologies from that of previous generations' digital immigrants. This dynamic is not likely to abate because, as Moore's law suggests, technology evolves rapidly and exponentially, with every future successive generation growing up in a world ever more altered by technological innovations.

This has profound implications for our entire educational system, including higher education. Some of the changes brought about by these technological innovations will be disruptive. Consequently, educators will need to scrutinize their own teaching practices and seek to align them with best practices in student learning. ILMs are one such technological innovation. These resources have the potential to address significant modern-day learning challenges such as student preparedness, student engagement, and attentiveness.

Interactive learning materials such as modules, games, and simulations are part of a rapidly expanding array of resources that educators will be able to access and use in their courses. Modules composed of both tutorials and practice exercises do not have a universally accepted design and development process or structure, which increases the gap between the development of poor- and high-quality tutorials. Key elements of a good module will include most (if not all) of Gagne's Nine Events of Instruction.

Learning games have been around for years, although only in the last decade has higher education been more open to accepting that games can be useful resources for educating students (Aldrich, 2009). Simulations have been used in higher education for several decades, but until recently the technology used to create them required a great deal of time, expertise, and money. In the future, the quantity and quality of all three types of ILMs will increase as these online educational resources are seen as aligning with successful pedagogy.

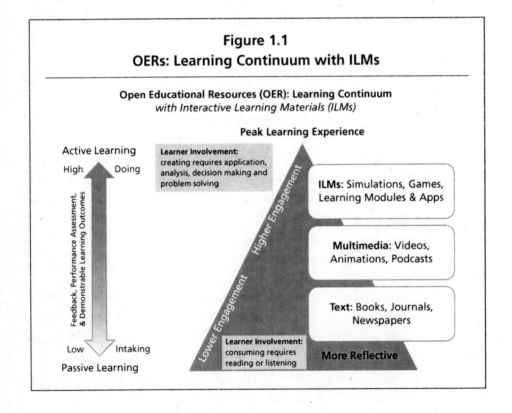

Figure 1.1
OERs: Learning Continuum with ILMs

A compelling case could be made to faculty to increasingly incorporate ILMs into their courses. Their design requires learner activity (both cognitive and physical) to progress through the resource. This built-in interactivity via practice exercises, gaming elements, and process simulation necessitates that learners become more engaged with the material if they are to complete it. Figure 1.1 illustrates that ILMs fall at the top of the learning continuum for OERs.

When students are engaged with educational resources on a high level, this can efficiently increase the amount of time they spend on task, which research has shown increases their curricular performance. Additionally, students can access ILMs using mobile computing devices wherever they are, which makes learning more convenient and accessible outside the classroom.

GOING FURTHER: RECOMMENDED READING

Digital Natives/Net Generation

Oblinger, D., and Oblinger, J. L. *Educating the Net Generation*. Boulder, CO: EDUCAUSE, 2005.

Palfrey, J. G, and Gasser, U. *Born Digital: Understanding the First Generation of Digital Natives*. New York: Basic Books, 2008.

Pew Research Center. "Internet & American Life Project Demographics Reports, 2000–12." http://pewinternet.org/Data-Tools/Get-the-Latest-Statistics/Latest-Research.aspx.

Prensky, M. *Teaching Digital Natives: Partnering for Real Learning*. Thousand Oaks, CA: Corwin, 2010.

Tapscott, D. *Grown Up Digital: How the Net Generation Is Changing Your World*. New York: McGraw-Hill, 2009.

Counterpoint Digital Natives/Net Generation

Bennett, S., Maton, K., and Kervin, L. "The 'Digital Natives' Debate: A Critical Review of the Evidence." *British Journal of Educational Technology*, 2008, 39(5), 775–786.

Helsper, E. J., and Eynon, R. "Digital Natives: Where Is the Evidence?" *British Educational Research Journal*, 2010, 36(3), 503–520.

Jones, C., Ramanau, R., Cross, S., and Healing, G. "Net Generation or Digital Natives: Is There a Distinct New Generation Entering University?" *Computers & Education*, 2010, 54(3), 722–732.

Kennedy, G. E., Judd, T. S., Churchward, A., Gray, K., and Krause, K. "First Year Students' Experiences with Technology: Are They Really Digital Natives." *Australasian Journal of Educational Technology*, 2008, 24(1), 108–122.

Educational Multimedia

Alessi, S. M., and Stanley, R. T. *Multimedia for Learning: Methods and Development.* Boston, MA: Allyn and Bacon, 2001.

Clark, R. C., and Mayer, R. E. *E-Learning and the Science of Instruction: Proven Guidelines for Consumers and Designers of Multimedia Learning.* San Francisco, CA: Pfeiffer, 2008.

Mayer, R. E. "The Promise of Multimedia Learning: Using the Same Instructional Design Methods across Different Media." *Learning and Instruction*, 2003, 13(2), 125–139.

Montgomery, S. "Addressing Diverse Learning Styles through the Use of Multimedia." Proceedings of the Frontiers in Education Conference, Las Vegas, NV, 1995.

Instructional Design and Technology

Dick, W., Carey, L., and Carey, J. O. *The Systematic Design of Instruction.* Upper Saddle River, NJ: Merrill/Pearson, 2009.

Gagné, R. M., Wager, W. W., Golas, K. C., and Keller, J. M. *Principles of Instructional Design.* Belmont, CA: Wadsworth, 2005.

Reiser, R. A., and Dempsey, J. *Trends and Issues in Instructional Design and Technology.* Boston, MA: Pearson, 2012.

Smith, P. L., and Ragan, T. J. *Instructional Design.* Hoboken, NJ: John Wiley & Sons, 2005.

Defining an Emergent Class of Educational Resources

Interactive Multimedia Modules, Simulations, and Games

If you don't know where you are going, you'll end up somewhere else.

— Yogi Berra

In the middle of a revolution, chaos tends to stir up a lot of dust that prevents us from clearly seeing what lies ahead. The information age is upon us. The digital revolution is changing both the ways we access information and the types of information we access. Computers allow us to create new forms of information that move beyond easy-to-grasp printed materials like books, magazines, and newspapers. These digital formats make it increasingly complex and difficult to discuss and define the emergence of new forms of educational resources such as interactive learning materials (ILMs). As the opening quote proclaims, if we do not know where we are going or what we are looking for, we will not likely know where we will end up or be able to locate what we are searching for. This means we need to gain a clear understanding of ILMs, in relationship to the universe of open educational resources (OERs), so that we can find what we are looking for — exactly the right ILM for our courses and students.

Simply taking the words individually (interactive + learning + materials), we could assume that any interactive content (i.e., not analog) used for learning might suffice as a working definition for ILMs. However, if this were the case, something as simple as an online puzzle of a math equation, a digital picture of a mountain landscape, or an online video describing how to solve the math equation would qualify as an ILM. A table of volcanic eruption dates from various national parks on a webpage in which you could input date rangers would fall into this category as well. However, even though these could be OERs and useful informational objects to assist students in learning new concepts and knowledge (i.e., they convey some type of basic data or information), they are not ILMs.

To successfully identify and find interactive learning materials, we must first define, as precisely and succinctly as possible, what these educational resources are. The first portion of this chapter presents a functional definition for ILMs that will be used throughout the remainder of the book, and the remaining text clarifies the nature and type of these educational resources.

INFORMATION HIERARCHY

Information scientists have hierarchically structured data, information, and knowledge from basic to more complex (Bellinger, Castro, and Mills, 2004). It is possible to similarly arrange these various types of learning objects on the Internet (Figure 2.1) so that they correspond to the structure of information as data object, informational object, and knowledge object (e.g., interactive learning materials).

This chart reflects that knowledge objects are at a higher level of information than data or informational objects. ILMs, like other knowledge objects, convey more than just data and information, although these are also part of their building blocks. As we learned through examining the instructional pedagogy of a learning module containing both tutorials and practice activities in the previous chapter, ILMs deliver instruction activities in a manner that data and information objects

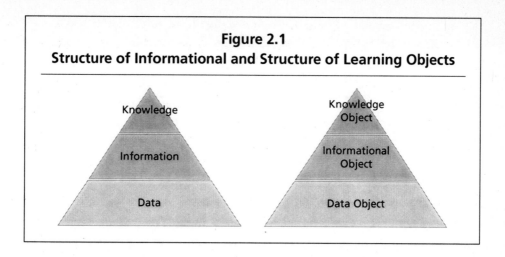

Figure 2.1
Structure of Informational and Structure of Learning Objects

Knowledge

Information

Data

Knowledge Object

Informational Object

Data Object

do not. Interactive learning materials should (1) be online resources that require more than a few minutes but no more than several hours to complete; (2) be designed to meet specific learning objectives (e.g., a lesson or topic); (3) include some type of learning or decision-making activity (e.g., practice and problem-solving exercises, process or tasks to complete, role-playing); and (4) guide students as well as provide them with feedback in the learning process. ILMs are discrete, content-specific resources designed to facilitate and improve student learning and retention.

We know that ILMs are OERs that provide instruction, although we could say the same thing about a digitized college textbook. So is a digital copy of a textbook that can be downloaded from Amazon.com an ILM? No. As discussed in the previous chapter, one of the most important components of an ILM is that it requires some level of decision-making for learners to advance through the material. The nature of these activities can vary greatly among the various types of ILMs, but they all involve learners in one or more of the following processes: applying, analyzing, and problem-solving.

Traditional textbooks require students to be only passive receptacles (i.e., to read) to receive the knowledge they contain and simply to turn the page to advance. This is not unlike a traditional lecture classroom, which requires students merely to sit back and passively listen as the instructor verbally—sometimes visually with PowerPoint—imparts knowledge to the class. In contrast, ILMs require students to be actively engaged with content by requiring them to perform some dynamic mental and physical actions to gain the information and receive feedback. The least desirable ILMs may require learners only to click on an icon to move through the content. By contrast, the most desirable may involve performing some higher-order actions that map well to the revised version of Bloom's taxonomy of educational objectives such as solving a problem, answering a question, or playing a game like a crossword puzzle (Pickard, 2007).

MORE THAN JUST WORDS

Additionally, online digital educational resources usually include multiple modalities and hypermedia to convey their contents. They frequently include some combination of audio, text, images (e.g., animations, pictures, graphics), and video. This means that ILMs are a derivation of multimedia not so unlike computer software programs. What sets ILMs apart from something like a flight training simulator software package or a game like SimCity is primarily in their size, scope, and dissemination. ILMs must have the ability simply to be shared and accessed with an Internet browser. In contrast, a flight simulator that trains student pilots to fly is very large in scope. The large size of this software and the scope of its learning objectives make it too large to be considered a type of chunkable online learning material. Furthermore, this software may not be able to be accessed from the Internet. If a specific learning objective or related set of objectives was extracted along with a related assessment instrument and a simulation was created to instruct a student on that discrete learning objective and only that portion was accessible to be integrated into a course via the Internet, then it would qualify as an ILM.

The definition is nearly complete. An ILM is a discrete digital, interactive, instructional resource used to teach a specific learning objective in a course or curriculum. The ability to openly share the resource across various courses synchronously regardless of location is the final missing component of the definition. Digital learning materials are composed of an increasing number of various digital, multimedia file types such as Hypertext Markup Language (HTML) script, Flash, JavaScript, Audio Video Interleave (AVI), Windows Media Video (WMV), MP3, and WAV. The digital components of ILMs are critical to allowing them to be shared over the Internet.

This brings us to our complete definition of what interactive learning materials are.

> An ILM is defined as any discrete online, interactive, instructional resource used to teach a specific learning objective (or small, related set of objectives).

The following definition identifies what an ILM is and what it is not, but to clarify how these resources facilitate student interaction it is necessary to identify the components that make up these resources. The previous chapter examined how Gagne's Nine Events of Instruction were incorporated into the design of the PSU Berks Calculus Modules to increase student engagement. Gagne's events work well for tutorials but not necessarily so for all educational games and simulations. The five elements that all types of ILMs must have to most effectively facilitate student interaction are the core content, hypermedia, decision-making activities, learner assessment, and feedback. The following graphic illustrates these elements (Figure 2.2).

Just as traditional printed materials are broken down into books, journals, magazines, and newspapers, several primary types of digital learning materials are being examined here. ILMs are educational resources such as online learning modules (that are primarily made up of interactive, multimedia tutorials often

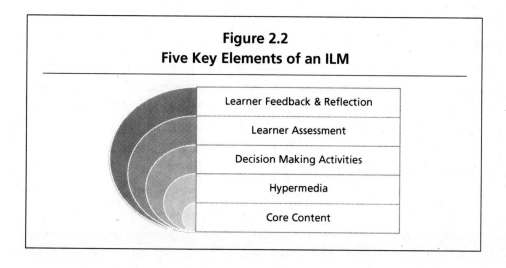

Figure 2.2
Five Key Elements of an ILM

Learner Feedback & Reflection

Learner Assessment

Decision Making Activities

Hypermedia

Core Content

containing interactive practice exercises and drills), educational simulations, and games. The following section examines the aforementioned types of ILMs to make this working definition more concrete.

MAKING IT PRACTICAL
Online Learning Modules: Interactive, Multimedia Tutorials with Exercises

The broadest of the three categories of ILMs are learning modules, which include multimedia tutorials with practice exercises and learning activities. As already examined in detail in the first chapter, educational modules with tutorials are often self-paced and provide guided learning exercises that teach by example and require learners to complete certain tasks as they progress. The sequence and structure of learning modules can vary greatly.

The most common sequence is linear (similar to reading a book from start to finish), where learners are expected to go step by step in a clearly identified progressive order (i.e., beginning to ending). The typical progression of tutorials is that they generally start with ". . . an introduction to the lesson and information is presented. Next, the learner answers a series of questions and the program evaluates them. Typical responses are 'sorry,' 'very good,' 'try again,' and 'right answer is,' among others. . . The cycle closes when the lesson is terminated, either by the learner or by the program. A summary appears at the close of the lesson" (Handal and Herrington, 2003, p. 280). The advantage to this approach is that students who need a more structured environment and guidance to cover all the important content and concepts will master them. It is possible for tutorials to be designed in a nonlinear fashion, which allows students to determine the sequence of steps and content they take and view. The advantage to this method is that it can encourage self-directed and inquiry-based learning (Lane and Cawley, 2001) as well as promote problem-solving.

The structure of most tutorials tends to be more personal and hierarchical. That is, as students progress through the tutorial, they are presented with more challenging content and activities that build on prior concepts and learning. This type of educational resource (unlike some games and simulations) is not well suited for groups or teams of students but is instead geared for individual students to use and go at their own learning pace.

Tutorials also include various interactive and multimedia elements and practice exercises to assess and reinforce student learning. Often these learning modules include activities like drill-and-practice exercises, which take a behaviorist approach and are geared toward helping students remember (i.e., memorize), demonstrate, and apply the content and knowledge they are learning in the module (Deubel, 2003).

Online Simulations: Almost the Real Thing

Computer simulations have been around for several decades now, and most people have used or are familiar with some type of computer software simulation. A Web-based simulation is similar to a computer software simulation but is accessible via the Internet. Both programs seek to imitate or represent a real-world process or situation and help learners to experience it virtually (Conrad and Donaldson, 2011). The primary function of a simulation generally does not include identically replicating a function, process, or system. Instead, it is goal oriented and should accurately depict the outcomes of a function, process, or system based on learners' actions and responses to what is being simulated.

This can be very useful in situations where it is not practical or safe for students to learn a process by actually performing it. For example, a flight simulator allows individuals who want to learn how to fly to experience what they will eventually experience when flying an actual plane but safely on the ground without the danger, added expense, or difficulty of gaining access to a plane. Because of the nature and complexity of most simulations, it is important for instructors to explain how the students in the course should use the simulation and to have a debriefing session with them after the activity is completed.

Online Games: Learning Should Be Fun, Shouldn't It?

Computer games have been around for years, but only within the last decade have they begun to be recognized as legitimate learning tools that can engage and enhance student learning in higher education. Web-based educational games instruct learners about a topic, concept, or problem in an interactive manner. They can motivate students to learn by offering them a fun, dynamic, and immersive environment where they often compete with themselves, with the game, with other peers, or with a combination of all three. Consequently, games can offer a more social constructivist approach to learning (Rieber, 1996; Dickey, 2005). These ILMs combine skill, competition, and at times chance, requiring learners to complete actions and tasks to advance, win, or otherwise successfully finish the game.

SYNOPSIS

Interactive learning materials are a class of resources geared for today's "Net generation" students, who seek to be actively engaged with whatever they are doing, including learning. These discrete online, interactive, instructional resources are used to teach a specific learning objective. They include educational modules, simulations, and games that are ideally suited to a generation of students who want the ease and convenience of accessing and doing their coursework whenever and wherever they can. To successfully complete the digital resource, ILMs necessitate that students focus their complete attention on their actions and use of the material.

As we will investigate in the later chapters of this book, educators can use these resources to support and reinforce classroom instruction either before or after class in addition to remediating and reminding students of important prior knowledge required for them to advance in their coursework. ILMs also can be useful for students who have missed class or need to review previous course content and themes individually at their own pace.

GOING FURTHER: RECOMMENDED READING

Digital Learning Materials

Bell, S. J., and Shank, J. *Academic Librarianship by Design: A Blended Librarian's Guide to the Tools and Techniques.* Chicago: American Library Association, 2007.

Educational Media, Games, and Simulations

Aldrich, C. *Learning Online with Games, Simulations, and Virtual Worlds: Strategies for Online Instruction.* San Francisco, CA: Jossey-Bass, 2009.

Alessi, S. M., and Trollip, S. R. *Computer-Based Instruction: Methods and Development* (2nd ed.). Englewood Cliffs, NJ: Prentice Hall, 1991.

Hertel, J. P., and Barbara, J. M. *Using Simulations to Promote Learning in Higher Education: An Introduction.* Sterling, VA: Stylus Pub, 2002.

Merrill, P. F., Hammons, K., Vincent, B. R., Reynolds, P. L., Christensen, L., and Tolman, M. N. *Computers in Education* (2nd ed.). Boston, MA: Allyn and Bacon, 1992.

Prensky, M. *Digital Game-Based Learning.* St. Paul, MN: Paragon House Publishers, 2007.

Schwier, R., and Misanchuk, E. R. *Interactive Multimedia Instruction.* Englewood Cliffs, NJ: Educational Technology Publications, 1993.

PART TWO

Finding ILMs: A Digital Exploration

Whoever starts out toward the unknown must consent to venture alone.

—Andre Gide

This section of the book will explore the multitude of different sites (e.g., digital repositories and libraries) as well as the search strategies and techniques that you can use to locate high-quality ILMs on the Internet. Like a ready reference sourcebook, it can be used independent from the rest of the book. Chapter 3 focuses on the best approach and techniques to make the search for high-quality modules and tutorials, simulations, and games more effective and efficient. The subsequent chapters will focus on a particular collection of sources: Chapter 4, international online educational repositories and libraries; Chapter 5, university and college repositories and sites;

Chapter 6, textbook publishers and entertainment media sites and collections; and Chapter 7, museums, professional organizations, and governmental organizations sites and collections. Each of these chapters will identify several of the very best sources to use in your search and will provide detailed information about how best to search each of these sources.

The Discovery Process
The Art of Discovering ILMs

*The greatest obstacle to discovery is not ignorance, it is the
illusion of knowledge.*

—Daniel Boorstin

The choice of the title for this chapter was very deliberate. The current environment makes it very challenging for educators and students alike to locate high-quality, appropriate interactive, digital learning materials. Over the course of the next decade, this process should become more straightforward and easier, but in the near future it will remain difficult. How faculty, librarians, instructional designers, and technologists go about finding good interactive learning materials (ILMs) is a process of discovery that is just as much art as science.

This chapter explores the search taxonomy (Figure 3.1) and process by which it is possible to locate high-quality and relevant ILMs from the numerous sources that create and provide access to them. Subsequent chapters explore in greater detail how to search specific online repositories, digital libraries, and websites.

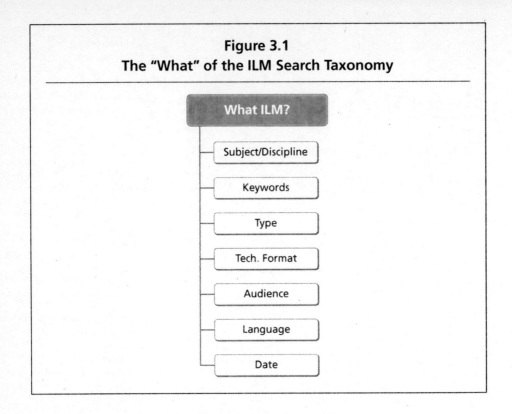

Figure 3.1
The "What" of the ILM Search Taxonomy

What ILM?

- Subject/Discipline
- Keywords
- Type
- Tech. Format
- Audience
- Language
- Date

IDENTIFING THE ILM SUBJECT AND KEYWORDS

As in conducting a search online for any type of information, it is critical to be able to clearly define and articulate what it is you want to find. This is perhaps even more essential in attempting to locate relevant ILMs because the standards for collecting and cataloging these types of materials are still not widely adopted (Figure 3.2). Begin with identifying the subject, topic, or discipline of the ILM you are looking for. It is better to start with the broadest subject matter to which the ILM relates and then to narrow it down to as specific a subject as possible.

This approach will allow you to start with the broadest set of related ILMs. Then by narrowing down its subject, topic, or discipline, you can develop a set of related keywords; if you have difficulty, use online tools like Google's Contextual Targeting Tool (formerly Wonder Wheel), which allows searchers to explore related terms in a format similar to mind-mapping software, which graphically displays related words and phrases (Mirizzi et al., 2010).

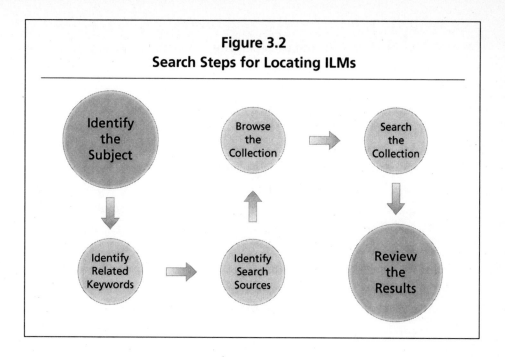

Figure 3.2
Search Steps for Locating ILMs

Identify the Subject

Browse the Collection

Search the Collection

Identify Related Keywords

Identify Search Sources

Review the Results

Determining the subject matter of the ILM is also critical because it will help to identity the sources that will best locate the resources, which is vital because you will never find what you are looking for if you are looking in the wrong places. For example, if you want to find an ILM on Spanish language grammar, you would want to eliminate the repositories that contain only the math and science resources.

The subsequent four chapters examine in great detail the very best sources you can search to locate ILMs. Furthermore, the best place to start your search is often with one of the large general collection digital repositories or digital libraries. These sites have the largest collections of ILMs and thereby increase the likelihood that you will find a relevant ILM. These sources can also be helpful in refining your search criteria.

BROWSING THE ILM COLLECTION

Browsing the collection of an online repository or digital library can be useful in helping to narrow down your search keywords and terms. For example, instructors who teach a basic or introductory chemistry course may want to help their students better understand gas laws. By going to a large online referatory such as MERLOT (McMartin, 2006) and using the browse function, it is possible to start with the broadest related category, Science & Technology, and then select Chemistry. In MERLOT the category Chemistry has nearly a thousand items. Not all of these are ILMs; rather, many are merely basic learning objects such as images, lessons, animations, and quizzes.

Within the Chemistry category, there are several possible options to locate a basic ILM for learning about the gas laws. You can select either Chemical Education or Introductory and General; these categories have some overlapping materials, with only about one hundred in Chemical Education and over three hundred in Introductory and General. If you select Chemical Education, the third result is Ideal Gas Law Simulation. If you select Introductory and General, Ideal Gas Law Simulation is the sixth result. To find more gas law ILMs, you would have to browse through the results of both categories, which could be very time-consuming, considering that there are over four hundred results in the aforementioned categories. Unlike most university libraries, which use Library of Congress subject headings to organize their collections, most online repositories and referatories do not use these headings. This results in very little consistency in subject headings across the various repositories, with the exception of some of the very broadest categories (e.g., math, science, history).

Quick Tip: *The browse function of most of the open educational repositories, libraries, and websites is best used when you do not have a very specific set of keywords that you have identified to locate your ILM. Also, when you are not finding many results, you can expand your search using this method.*

SEARCHING THE ILM COLLECTION

As mentioned previously, it is often essential to identify relevant keywords or phrases that describe the desired ILMs because it is not always possible or efficient to use subject or discipline classifications for locating these online educational resources. However, using highly relevant and specific words is not always as simple as it might seem. A number of basic and advanced search techniques

Table 3.1
Rudimentary Primer on Search Operators
(Search Techniques)

Common Keyword Search Operators	Result
AND	This will return only results that have both words occurring in the Title, Subject Heading, or Description. This is useful to narrow down results.
OR	This will return results that have either word occurring in the Title, Subject Heading, or Description. This is useful to expand the number of results.
NOT	This will return only results that do not contain the word following NOT in the Title, Subject Heading, or Description. This is useful to limit the number of results, especially if one of the search words is associated with another topic that is not desired.
*	This commonly used truncation symbol will find key words that contain various ending of a word (e.g., gas, gases, gassing, gassed).
"Quotes"	This allows you to search the exact word phrase.
NEAR	This allows you to search words that occur near but not next to each other.

and options may be available, depending on the online source being searched (Table 3.1).

Using the previous example, if you were to have simply typed "gas laws" into the simple search box located at the top of MERLOT's website, you would have less than a dozen results. However, none of these six results are the Ideal Gas Law Simulation that we discovered in browsing the MERLOT subject heading categories. This is because, like most keyword search strings, it returns results for the exact matches of the text, in this case the words "gas" and "laws." Because the aforementioned simulation does not have the letter "s" in the word "law," it does not come to the top of the search query. Performing the keyword search with "gas law" returns a total of more than twenty results, and Ideal Gas Law Simulation is the first listed result.

Most online repositories, referatories, and digital libraries have advanced search options as well, which allow you to either expand or narrow down your results to increase the possibility of finding an appropriate ILM. Using search operators is part art and part science. Table 3.1 lists the most common search operators and their functions, which are available when searching the vast majority of online repositories and digital libraries.

The basic search box allows you to do a quick and simple keyword search, which is best for finding the largest quantity instead of the most precise listing of results. Consequently, when searching a source that does not include hundreds or thousands of results, this type of search is recommended. For example, if the source you are searching lists that it has a collection of only several dozen calculus ILMs, the best approach to finding a relevant educational resource (avoiding inadvertently excluding any) would either be to simply browse the listed collection or to do a simple keyword search for the desired ILM.

Nearly all online repositories and libraries include more advanced search functions that allow you to narrow down, refine, and improve the precision of your search. Because the advanced search function varies widely among the different online resources, Chapter 4 elaborates on how to use the advanced search options for each of the resources. It is useful to understand some of the noteworthy aspects of ILMs that can aid you in searching for a specific genre type (i.e., module/tutorial, simulation, or game) or technology format (e.g., Adobe Flash).

THE TYPE OF ILM

Identifying the type of digital learning material is essential because this should directly correspond to instructional goals and course learning objectives. If you want to expose students to a topic or concept, an educational tutorial that provides a sequential, detailed overview might be more appropriate than first having them use a simulation. However, a simulation that allows students to practice or virtually experience a process that they have already been exposed to can reinforce their learning and make it more concrete.

Additionally, the amount of interactivity and level of instructional components that are present often correspond to ILM type, or genre of the online resource, such as complex interactive animations, instructional simulations, online tutorials, modules, educational games, or interactive multimedia presentations. Games offer a highly interactive and engaging experience that tests students' ability to demonstrate what has been learned and provides additional practice to reinforce learning.

By identifying the type of educational resource, you can search specifically for just that kind of ILM. In the Ideal Gas Law Simulation example, it would be possible to limit your results to return only ILMs that are simulations. This can allow you to quickly narrow down the list of ILMs you are searching through.

THE ILM FORMAT

The format — that is, the digital foundation or computer programming language or software platform of the technology on which the ILM is built — is very important because some software technologies will not work on some hardware platforms. Apple's very popular iPhone and iPod Touch will not support or play Adobe Flash. Currently, this presents some big challenges because one of the primary technologies used to create educational tutorials is Adobe Flash.

Some of the more popular technological formats that already exist are Sun's (now Oracle's) Java, Apple's QuickTime, and Microsoft's PowerPoint, and even more are constantly being created and developed. Increasingly, Web browser application-based formats are being developed to allow students to use tutorials, games, and simulations by simply downloading a plug-in. These Web-based formats will likely become the standard by which we access applications via the Web through increasingly more popular cloud computing.

The format can be useful in searching for ILMs because it can help to limit search results as well as to find a particular kind of educational resource. For example, a librarian may want to locate a tutorial that will expose students to a particular aspect of information literacy such as evaluating sources on the Internet. If the librarian uses the advanced search function to limit the results to a specific file format (e.g., Adobe Flash file format), this increases the likelihood of finding a tutorial in which students can progress as they successfully demonstrate the important components in evaluating Internet resources. A good example of this is the modules of Texas Information Literacy Tutorial (TILT) (Orme, 2004).

THE ILM AUDIENCE

To locate the most appropriate ILM, it is essential to determine the audience level. This is especially true when looking for an educational resource that will be best suited for the students in your course. Some ILMs would be appropriate for both upper-level high school and lower-level college students, and others are suitable only for a very specific group, such as upper-level baccalaureate students. Many repositories and digital libraries will allow searchers to focus their search for a specified level or audience, while other resources (e.g., search engines) will not. By using this limiter when available, a searcher can quickly narrow down the relevant results.

THE ILM LANGUAGE

The language component of the ILM is straightforward. The vast majority of interactive learning materials created in the United States, Canada, Australia, and the United Kingdom are in English. However, many other non-English-speaking countries are developing ILMs. Especially for students who are learning a foreign language, finding ILMs in the language in which they are studying can be very helpful. When available, limiting a search for a specific language (other than English) can help to efficiently limit the returned results of ILMs.

THE ILM CURRENCY (DATE, TIMELINESS)

An ILM's authored or creation date can be vital in determining the appropriateness of the discovered resource. Many times ILMs will not specifically identify the creation date, but most do include a copyright, which provides a basic reference point for the currency of the resource. Knowing the timeliness of an ILM is most important in the science and technology fields where new knowledge changes rapidly and can impact the understanding of knowledge within the field. In the aforementioned fields, using the date criterion when searching for desired digital learning materials can help to quickly narrow down the relevant results.

WHERE TO FIND ILMS

There are a multitude of places online to search for educational digital learning materials. Not surprisingly, if you are not familiar with the sources, it often is not a simple task to determine the best starting point to target the search (Figure 3.3).

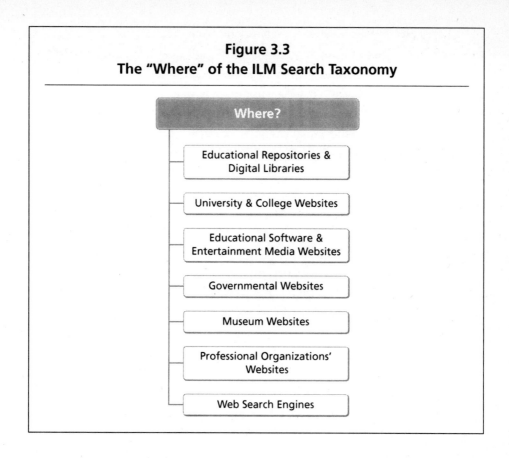

Figure 3.3
The "Where" of the ILM Search Taxonomy

Where?

- Educational Repositories & Digital Libraries
- University & College Websites
- Educational Software & Entertainment Media Websites
- Governmental Websites
- Museum Websites
- Professional Organizations' Websites
- Web Search Engines

A good practice until you become more familiar with an online resource is to start with a general repository or digital library that focuses on collecting, housing, or referring to online educational learning materials.

As mentioned earlier, Web-based repositories and digital libraries either house the ILMs or simply link or point to the resources. One of the advantages of repositories, which contain their collections, over referatories, which simply link to the online educational resources, is that the former have greater control over their materials. The latter are more prone to having broken and obsolete links (Shank, 2003).

General education repositories and referatories such as Wisconsin Online and MERLOT are often good starting points for locating ILMs on general topics and are appropriate for high school and college students. They are usually well organized and easy to search and contain thousands of ILMs. Discipline-specific online libraries like NSDL focus on math and sciences.

Colleges and universities have increasingly been creating and making ILMs freely available. These resources are often very high quality and appropriate for high school honor students and seniors as well as all undergraduate college students. Most higher education institutions do not have nearly the extensive collections that the general resource sites do. Additionally, the different terminologies they use can make them more challenging to access and search. For example, Penn State University refers to its ILMs as multimedia teachable objects (MTOs) (Penn State University Information Technology Services, 2009).

Educational software and entertainment media companies are increasingly developing ILMs because they have picked up on the trend that the younger generation likes and wants to be able to access these types of resources. For-profit educational software companies do not give away very many learning modules with tutorials and exercises, simulations, and games since they would not be able to remain in business by doing so. Likewise, educational publishers such as McGraw-Hill, Pearson, and Wiley do not make their digital educational resources available except through supplemental content intended for their textbooks. Instructors who select and use these textbooks often do have access to the corresponding ILMs and can make them available to students in their courses through a learning management system such as Blackboard.

Museums and entertainment media companies like Discovery Channel and PBS create high-quality and freely available ILMs, but it can be challenging to locate these unless you know a specific museum exhibit or TV program. Government organizations like NASA also provide free and well-made ILMs, but since there is no federally mandated approach to making government resources searchable they can be difficult to locate, too.

Professional organizations have sponsored, created, or indexed ILMs that they have determined benefit their profession. For example, PRIMO (Peer-Reviewed Instructional Materials Online), offered by the American Association of College and Research Libraries, allows librarians to search to find library instruction and informing literacy tutorials. Web search engines like Google and Bing can be useful in finding that diamond in the rough but should be employed only as a last resort because it requires a great deal of time and effort to locate a high-quality ILM using these search sites.

Becoming familiar with the various categories of ILM resources (the "where" portion of the taxonomy) can make finding high-quality and appropriate resources much easier.

REVIEWING THE RESULTS

Not all ILMs are created equal. Interactive learning materials, like any other resource, have varying degrees of quality. However, unlike books, ILMs have a number of additional instructional components beyond the content. Before instructors adopt these resources, it is important that they use three main areas of selection criteria—content, engagement, and design (CED)—to evaluate the quality of the identified ILMs.

Obviously, content should be king. If the information contained in the ILM is inaccurate, then the rest of the ILM is useless. Also, the author and publisher information can inform the instructor's opinion of how authoritative the resource is and what its bias might be.

The degree and type of interaction can vary greatly, especially among the various types of ILMs (i.e., tutorials, simulations, and games). This is an important component because students' level of engagement can be directly impacted by how much interaction they have to perform to progress through the resource. The amount and quality of engagement can influence and impact the time students spend using the ILM. As mentioned in the previous chapter, research has shown that higher levels of time involved with course content lead to greater student course success (i.e., higher GPA and better information retention) (Amaral and Shank, 2010).

Tutorials tend to have less interaction than games and simulations. However, not all educational games have interactions that instructors or students will find engaging or resonate with. A game that is in the format of a game show will appeal to a different audience than a game that is in a role-playing style. The quality of interactions in simulations is extremely important. Simulations that do not have authentic interactions that closely or accurately mimic the real world are likely to be less effective in helping students relate to it.

While the design of a book is important, the design of an ILM is absolutely critical. ILMs are more complex to create than books because the content, engagement, interface, media, pedagogy, and technology all have to fit seamlessly and ubiquitously together. When selecting this type of resource, each of the aforementioned components needs to be critically examined.

We have already discussed content and engagement, but the interface design can make or break an ILM. A poor user interface design can ruin an otherwise good resource. Fortunately, it is fairly easy to spot a poorly designed interface. If you have difficulty learning to use or navigate the resource, then your students are likely to as well. ILMs that make extensive use of high-quality multimedia are also good candidates to incorporate into your course. The power of using different forms of media is that they can resonate with diverse learning styles. ILMs that have limited media or poor quality and are difficult to see, hear, or read have limited effectiveness.

The principles, strategies, and methods of instruction (i.e., pedagogy) incorporated into ILMs can also impact the effectiveness of student learning. Additionally, it can be difficult to determine the pedagogical approach the digital learning material takes to assist students in learning the content. Generally, the pedagogy of simulations and games is easier to evaluate because simply playing the game or working through the simulation gives a clear impression of the instructional strategy. Tutorials are more difficult to judge, but as we saw in Chapter 1 they can be very important. The technology used to create the ILM is essential as well. Critically ask yourself: Is the technology going to provide access to or inhibit students' ability to use the resource?

SYNOPSIS

This chapter covers the primary search techniques and the most important general guidelines that you will need to consider when you are looking for any type of interactive learning material. First, you need to clearly decide *what* you are looking for considering the subject or discipline. Determine what is the most applicable classification or topic for the ILM. Second, brainstorm a list of keywords that most accurately describe the ILM. Third, decide what type of ILM you are looking for: a module or tutorial; simulation, or game. Fourth, consider if specific software such as Adobe Flash or JavaScript is used to create the ILM. Fifth, determine what type of student (i.e., grade, skill level) will use the ILM. Sixth, decide on the ILM's native language based on who will be using it. And last, based on the ILM's publication date, decide how relevant it is to the topic you will be teaching.

Then after determining the ILM's criteria, decide *where* to begin your search. Consider the size of the repository or resource as well as its focus. A good practice is to begin with casting the widest net and then to narrow your results to increase your precision. Consider searching nonprofit educational repositories and libraries; college and university websites; educational publishers, media, and entertainment sites; government organizations; museums; nonprofit professional organizations; and Web search engines based on which category of site best fits the subject or topic of your search. Then review the list of returned results from the sources you searched, considering content, engagement, and design: How accurate, authoritative, relevant, and appropriate is the ILM for your students? What is the level (the higher the better) of the actions, activities, exercises, and assessments the ILM requires students to perform? How appealing is the ILM to use, how much multimedia is embedded into it, how easy is it to use, and how much control and flexibility does it give learners?

GOING FURTHER: RECOMMENDED READING

Aldrich, C. *Learning Online with Games, Simulations, and Virtual Worlds: Strategies for Online Instruction.* San Francisco, CA: Jossey-Bass, 2009.

Bell, S. J., and Shank, J. *Academic Librarianship by Design: A Blended Librarian's Guide to the Tools and Techniques.* Chicago: American Library Association, 2007.

The Pioneers

Searching Online Educational Repositories in North America and the United Kingdom

> *The task of the leader is to get his people from where they are to where they have not been.*
>
> —Henry Kissinger

Leading the way is never easy. You have to blaze your own trail and overcome all types of unexpected obstacles. In the past decade, there have been a number of failed attempts to create large, multidiscipline online repositories or libraries that collect various types of interactive learning materials. The ones discussed in this chapter are the surviving pioneers that set out to collect and make open educational resources (OERs) — including interactive learning materials (ILMs) — widely available. As we shall see, they all are unique in the paths they took. Overall, the resources listed here are the very best of the large, multidiscipline repositories and referatories and are considered the best and most stable. This chapter explores several of the largest and highest quality sources from North America, Europe, and the United Kingdom.

If you need to quickly identify a good starting source to look for ILMs, use the Quick Start Guide (Table 4.1), which lists the best repositories for the various major disciplines in academia. This chapter also includes detailed information about each of the repositories, including their strengths and weaknesses and detailed descriptions of how to most effectively and efficiently search each one. This chapter also contains Web links to an ILM clearinghouse with timely, short instructional videos that provide directions on the best search strategies and techniques to use for each of the sources covered in this chapter (Table 4.2).

SEARCH STRATEGY

When you have well-defined and specific terminology and keywords for the resource you are looking for, generally you will want to do a keyword search. The basic search for most repositories works well (especially when you are focusing on returning the most possible relevant results). If you have a subject or topic that is going to return a large number of results, then using the advanced search function of a repository is the most efficient and effective method to start your search.

When you do not have well-defined and specific terminology or are not quite certain what type of ILM you want to locate, the browse function of the repositories is often the best starting point. This will often return a larger number of results and can be very useful for locating resources that you might have missed if you had performed a keyword search. The downside of using this approach is that it generally takes you more time to locate relevant ILMs.

NORTH AMERICA
MERLOT

MERLOT (Multimedia Educational Resource for Learning and Online Teaching; http://www.merlot.org/) was started in 1997. It is the oldest and one of the largest general repositories in existence today. Because it is a repository, it houses only

Table 4.1
Quick Start Guide for Selecting Repositories by Subject

By Major Discipline/Subject	Best Starting Point	Good Alternatives
Arts		
Architecture	OER Commons	MERLOT/NSDL
Art History	MERLOT	OER Commons/NCLOR
Fine Arts	MERLOT	OER Commons/NCLOR
Music	MERLOT	OER Commons
Photography	OER Commons	MERLOT
Theatre	Jorum	MERLOT/OER Commons
Business		
Accounting	MERLOT	OER Commons/Wisc-Online
Economics	MERLOT	OER Commons/Jorum
Finance	OER Commons	MERLOT/Jorum
Information Systems	MERLOT	Jorum/OER Commons
Management	MRELOT	OER Commons/Wisc-Online
Marketing	MERLOT	OER Commons
Humanities		
Communication Studies	MERLOT	OER Commons
English	MERLOT	OER Commons
History	MERLOT	OER Commons/NCLOR
Philosophy	MERLOT	OER Commons
Religious Studies	MERLOT	OER Commons
Women and Gender Studies	MERLOT	OER Commons
World Languages	MERLOT	OER Commons
Math		
Mathematics	NSDL	MERLOT/OER Commons
Statistics and Probability	NSDL	MERLOT/OER Commons
Science and Technology		
Agriculture Sciences	NSDL	MERLOT/OER Commons
Astronomy	NSDL	MERLOT/OER Commons
Biology & Anatomy	NSDL	MERLOT/Wisc-Online
Chemistry	NSDL	MERLOT/OER Commons

(continued)

Table 4.1
Quick Start Guide for Selecting Repositories by Subject
(*continued*)

By Major Discipline/Subject	Best Starting Point	Good Alternatives
Computer Science	NSDL	MERLOT/OER Commons
Engineering	NSDL	OER Commons/MERLOT
Geoscience	NSDL	OER Commons/MERLOT
Health Sciences	MERLOT	NSDL/OER Commons
Information Technology	Jorum	OER Commons/MERLOT
Physics	NSDL	MERLOT/OER Commons
Social Sciences		
Anthropology	NSDL	MERLOT/OER Commons
Criminal Justice & Law	MERLOT	Jorum/OER Commons
Geography	OER Commons	NSDL/MERLOT
Political Science	MERLOT	OER Commons/NSDL
Psychology	MERLOT	OER Commons/NSDL
Sociology	MERLOT	OER Commons/NSDL

the records of the learning materials, not the actual materials. Table 4.3 provides a list of MERLOT's key features. It was conceived at the California State University Center for Distributed Learning and has evolved into a partnership including the University of Georgia System, Oklahoma State Regents for Higher Education, University of North Carolina System, and the California State University System. This consortium of large and well-funded institutions means that MERLOT is one of the most stable and financially sound OER sites.

MERLOT II launched in October 2013 and continues to evolve as institutional partners and professional organizations are invited to join the cooperative endeavor. It is a freely available resource designed primarily for faculty and students in higher education, but it also has materials for grades K–12. It links to all types of online learning materials (i.e., a referatory) and thus provides basic descriptions along with annotations, which include peer reviews (Table 4.3). MERLOT provides access to many types of online learning materials such

Table 4.2
Video List for Searching Nonprofit Online Educational Repositories/Libraries

	Video URL
MERLOT: Browsing	http://infogr.am/MERLOT-Browsing-the-Collection
MERLOT: Basic Searching	http://infogr.am/MERLOT-Basic-Search-Searching-the-Collection/
MERLOT: Advanced Searching	http://infogr.am/MERLOT-Advanced-Search-Searching-the-Collection
OER Commons: Browsing	http://infogr.am/OER-Commons-Browsing-the-Collection/
OER Commons: Basic Searching	http://infogr.am/OER-Commons-Basic-Search-Searching-the-Collection/
OER Commons: Advanced Searching	http://infogr.am/OER-Commons-Advanced-Search-Searching-the-Collection/
ARIADNE: Browsing	http://infogr.am/ARIADNE-Browsing-the-Collection/
ARIADNE: Searching	http://infogr.am/ARIADNE-Basic-Search-Searching-the-Collection/
JORUM: Browsing	http://infogr.am/JORUM-Browsing-the-Collection/
JORUM: Basic Searching	http://infogr.am/JORUM-Basic-Search-Searching-the-Collection/
JORUM: Advanced Searching	http://infogr.am/JORUM-Advanced-Search-Searching-the-Collection/

as presentations, quizzes and tests, animations, lesson plans, and ILMs (i.e., educational tutorials, simulations, and games).

The Collection (Quality, Usability, Currency, Reliability) MERLOT is one of the largest referatories on the Web. Its collections were built by a community

Table 4.3
MERLOT Features Overview

Subject Areas	Arts, business, education, humanities, math, science and technology, social sciences
Collection Size	40,000+
Collection Type	17 types including tutorials and simulations
Collection Nature	Referatory
Access (free/fee membership)	Free, membership available not required
Editorial/Review	Peer reviewed/volunteer contributed

of more than 100,000, most of whom initially were involved in higher education (i.e., faculty, librarians, and faculty support personnel). Increasingly, K–12 educators have joined in the effort. Contributors volunteer their time to submit materials and to review resources for MERLOT.

With more than 40,000 materials, MERLOT contains hundreds, if not thousands, of ILMs. Many of the community members are professionals in their disciplinary fields, which often makes the materials they add and review of high quality. Additionally, to help searchers find the most appropriate resources, MERLOT allows peer review of the materials submitted. Members have to be trained and approved to become peer evaluators, and then they can evaluate materials in their specific discipline or areas of expertise and give a 1- to 5-star rating as well as provide a detailed review. Furthermore, MERLOT awards the best and highest quality materials with a MERLOT Classics or Editors' Choice Award.

The content of the tutorials, simulations, and games created by faculty and college and university instructional staff is often very accurate. The depth of coverage can vary greatly across all the categories of materials. High school seniors and honor students as well as college undergraduate students can use a great deal of introductory and general education materials. The ILM design often varies in quality far more than the accuracy of the content. This is because the materials are being created by all types of faculty and support staff, some of whom have a great deal of design and development expertise and others of whom have very little. Likewise, the level of engagement built into the ILMs varies greatly, especially in the area of tutorials. Tutorials on the low end of engagement might require the learner to simply navigate to advance the content; as discussed earlier, this low level of engagement is closer to the passive learning side of the OER continuum and thus is the least desirable sort of ILM.

The strength of MERLOT—its community members—can also be its weakness. The members contribute all of the materials in the collection. Therefore, the collection is only as strong as its community members. All community members can make comments on any of the material in the collections no matter what level of expertise they have. This means they can also comment on their own contributions, which potentially creates conflicts of interest (e.g., Penn State Berks CLT—Team Dynamics and Building record in MERLOT; http://www.merlot .org/merlot/viewMaterial.htm?id=531495).

MERLOT does not have a great deal of control over the usability of the materials it collects. This is a result of merely providing a link to the vast majority of the content in the repository. However, it attempts to help searchers identify the technical format as well as the type of platform with which the material works. The ease with which instructors can integrate the materials into their course depends on the technology that they have available to them. Learning management systems like Blackboard can make material integration easier.

The currency of the material could become a greater issue as time passes since MERLOT has been in existence for less than two decades. In the areas of general education math and humanities, this is of less concern since the basic foundation knowledge changes very little over time in these fields. However, in the sciences, material timeliness could become problematic as new theories and knowledge replace or change current understandings. To address this shortfall, MERLOT recently created the date fields "added to MERLOT" and last "modified in MER-LOT." Many of the materials also include copyright dates.

Users could also encounter issues with links to material on MERLOT since the website does not directly house the material. For example, if the server on which the material is stored is down, then the link will not work. Also, if the material's URL changes at the host site, it will not be automatically updated in MERLOT and may not work unless the author of the material updates the new link. MERLOT has attempted to remedy this by including a "Report Broken Link" button on every record; anyone (including nonmembers) can click this to notify the webmaster that a link is not working.

Searchability MERLOT's collections can be searched quite easily using subject browsing, a basic search box, and an advanced material search tool. The following sections provide detailed information on how to effectively use each of the three search functions.

Browsing The browsing function is straightforward and simple to use (click here to view the Browsing MERLOT video; http://infogr.am/MERLOT-Browsing-the-Collection). From the main webpage of MERLOT click on "Search MERLOT" and then "Browse All Materials." Users can select one of eight main subject headings in addition to Academic Support Services. Selecting the Business category then leads to several layers of subcategories. For example, the following path can be taken to find a tutorial on teamwork: "Browse Path: All > Business > Management > Org Behavior and Development." Generally, there are one to three subcategories per each main heading. The number of subcategories is a real strength for MERLOT. It allows users to refine their search and makes browsing the collection easier.

MERLOT provides the complete path taken when browsing the collection. This search trail allows you to orient yourself within the collection and to easily jump back to a previous category. As you browse through the collection, you are able to select the type of material you desire. The material types are dependent on their availability in selected categories.

The browse collection function works well when you are not certain exactly what you are looking for. Also, you may come across results that you would miss if you conducted a keyword search and left out specific words that would have identified the material. Furthermore, browsing the collection is very useful in narrowing down your results. If you already are fairly certain what you are looking for and have some keywords selected, the browse function is not the best option because it generally is not as efficient and quick as a keyword search.

Basic Search The basic search is a simple keyword search tool located at the top right corner of the website. Typing in keywords related to the material you are looking for will return results. After doing this, you will get a list of results in the center of the search results page. You can then choose how you would like to display your results (i.e., relevance, overall rating, title, author, material type [alphabetical order], date added, date modified). On the top left side of this page, you will see the main subject categories that have materials containing the keywords (click here to view the Searching MERLOT video; http://infogr.am/MERLOT-Basic-Search-Searching-the-Collection/). Directly below you are shown the types of materials that contain the keywords. At the very bottom of the left side your recent keyword search terms are displayed.

Quick Tip: MERLOT does not recognize AND, OR, and NOT; rather, it uses + and –. Using the minus sign will exclude any term from appearing in the results, which usually will expand the number of results. Combining the terms and searching "teamwork" will return some different results from searching for "team work" because in MERLOT's keyword search it is looking for the exact search string. It is possible to use quotation marks in the basic search to find the exact word phrase you are searching for. This technique tends to help find more precise results and limits the number of results you get.

This is normally not the most precise method for finding your material. The search box automatically treats multiple keywords with the AND (i.e., +) search operator. This means that it will return results that have only both terms appearing in their record. Consequently, a search of "team work" or "team + work" returns exactly the same results.

The basic search function works best with materials that you have a clear understanding of and from which you know pertinent, specific keywords. Additionally, general materials that fit neatly under main subject headings can be found quickly using the basic search. The basic search will usually return the most results within MERLOT. It is possible to combine the keyword search with the browse function by first searching specific keywords (e.g., "team work") and then using the navigation bar results to narrow down your results to find the material you need.

Advanced Search If precision is what you desire when searching MERLOT, then using the advanced search function is your best option. However, the complexity and time it takes to use this function is far greater than that of using the basic search or simply browsing the collection. To access the Advanced Search Materials Search tool, click on the link below the materials search box on MERLOT's main webpage.

The Advanced Material Search page allows you to search several ways (i.e., any words, all words, and exact phrase) and to select different criteria (e.g., "subject category," "language," "material type," "technical format") to return more precise results (click here to view the Advanced Searching MERLOT video; http://infogr.am/MERLOT-Advanced-Search-Searching-the-Collection). It is possible to combine keywords with words that appear in the title of the material or even the description. The keyword field will give you the largest quantity of results because it looks for keywords in multiple fields including the title and description.

Quick Tip: Searching only the title or description fields will limit the number of results returned from your search while not necessarily increasing the precision of your search.

The challenge in using the advanced search function is that while using the drop-down boxes to select specific criteria to return the most precise search results you may inadvertently end up limiting the results and missing some very appropriate, high-quality materials. The reason for this is that the materials are cataloged by the individuals who submit them. Consequently, they differ widely in the consistency of the bibliographic information.

A good example of this is the "Team Dynamics and Building" tutorial, which is classified under the material type of tutorial but also contains drill and practice exercises. Nevertheless, if you were not familiar with this tutorial you would have no way of knowing this. Consequently, searching by limiting your results to material types that are classified as drill and practice exercises would exclude this tutorial.

Similarly, the tutorial was created in Adobe Flash. This is listed in the description portion of the record but not in the technical format section. If you were doing a search for tutorials about team building and limited the results to only those listing Adobe Flash in the technical format section, then you would be excluding the "Team Dynamics and Building" tutorial.

The Final Verdict It is not by mistake that MERLOT II was the first of the repositories examined in this book. It is currently one of the biggest and easiest repositories in which to search for ILMs among other OERs. This should be

Table 4.4
MERLOT Evaluation Scorecard

Five Criteria	Rating (1 Low—5 High)
Collection	****
Validity	****
Significance/Coverage	*****
Design	****
Engagement	***
Searchability	****
Browsing	*****
Searching	****
Usability	****
Currency	***
Reliability	****
Overall Score	****

considered a must-search repository for instructors looking for high-quality ILMs to integrate into their courses. MERLOT covers most disciplines very well, especially for general introductory college courses. This repository should be the first or one of the first searched. With this in mind, no repository is large enough at this point to be the only source used when searching for relevant high-quality interactive learning materials. As discussed earlier, MERLOT is not perfect, and there are both benefits and drawbacks to relying on volunteer members to contribute materials. It is also noteworthy that MERLOT is trying to address accessibility issues (i.e., for visually or hearing impaired individuals) by adding a field that allows the contributor to identify if the material is accessible and to what degree. Table 4.4 indicates MERLOT's strengths and weaknesses.

Going Further: Recommended Reading

Cafolla, R. "Project Merlot: Bringing Peer Review to Web-Based Educational Resources." *Journal of Technology and Teacher Education*, 2006, 14(2), 313–323.

Cechinel, C., and Sánchez-Alonso, S. "Analyzing Associations between the Different Ratings Dimensions of the MERLOT Repository." *Interdisciplinary Journal of E-Learning and Learning Objects*, 2011, 7, 1–10.

Malloy, T. E., and Hanley, G. L. "MERLOT: A Faculty-Focused Web Site of Educational Resources." *Behavior Research Methods, Instruments, & Computers: A Journal of the Psychonomic Society*, 2001, 33(2), 274–276.

OER COMMONS

The Open Educational Resources Commons (http://www.oercommons.org/) was created by the Institute for the Study of Knowledge Management in Education (ISKME) in 2007 with funding provided by the William and Flora Hewlett Foundation. It functions as a portal for teaching and learning materials around the world. The site integrates Web 2.0 technologies that enable social bookmarking, tagging, rating, and reviewing. The overall collection size is slightly larger than that of MERLOT's (roughly 60,000 materials, only 27,000 of which are geared for postsecondary students). It is growing rapidly because of alliances it is forging with over 120 content partners (e.g., MIT OpenCourseWare, Internet Archive, Connexions). Like with MERLOT, it is also possible to freely search the OER collections. Furthermore, educators can join the community to participate in contributing, tagging, rating, and reviewing items.

Table 4.5
OER Commons Features Overview Chart

Subject Areas	Arts, business, humanities, math and statistics, science and technology, and social sciences
Collection Size	55,000+
Collection Type	17 types including games, interactive, and simulations
Collection Nature	Metasearch referatory
Access (free/fee membership)	Free, membership available—not required
Editorial/Review	Peer reviewed/volunteer contributed

The Collection (Quality, Usability, Currency, and Reliability) OER Commons has been in existence less than five years and already is one of the largest repositories on the Web. It contains an international collection of resources assembled both by building relationships with content partners (i.e., public, private organizations, companies, school districts, and higher education institutions) and by allowing community members (i.e., instructors, students, self-learners, researchers, administrators, and content providers) who are involved in primary, secondary, and higher education to contribute materials and review resources.

Similar to MERLOT, not all the resources in the OER Commons are ILMs. The OER Commons does contain numerous games, simulations, and interactive resources along with instructional materials, some of which are tutorials and learning modules. The affiliations with respectable content partners such as MIT also attest to the high quality of many of the materials in the OER Commons. The OER Commons has staff dedicated to reviewing and approving all the materials submitted by individual members. Moreover, it allows members to rate (on a scale of 1 to 5 stars) and review all materials.

OER Commons has a large percentage of materials for primary, secondary, and postsecondary educators. The depth of coverage, as a result, can vary greatly. Similar to MERLOT, the design of the ILMs in the OER Commons often varies in quality far more than the accuracy of the content, although some of its partners provide very high design quality for their games and simulations. This repository does not have a separate category for tutorials (although they could fall under the general material type category of "Other"); therefore, it can be more challenging to locate them.

The strength of OER Commons is in the partnerships it is forming with large content providers. This potentially can allow the repository to continue to grow its collections very quickly. Also, the quality of the content provided from its partners is generally very good. Like with MERLOT, community members can also contribute materials to OER Commons, and as a result the consistency of the cataloging records can vary greatly. Additionally, a large percentage of the materials are not rated or commented on.

Because the OER Commons is a Web portal and its collections only refer to (and do not house) materials, it does not have control over the usability of the materials to which it links. It does identify the media format but not the technical format of the material in its records. Determining the currency of the material in the OER Commons is challenging because no date information is available in the record citations. This should not be a problem in fields like basic math, where foundational knowledge changes little. However, in areas like science and technology, material could become outdated and inaccurate.

Just like MERLOT, OER Commons simply links to the material in its collections; thus, the reliability of the links can vary widely. However, during the review of this repository no broken links were observed, which seems to indicate that the OER staff and its affiliated partners do a good job of fixing broken links. Surprisingly, the OER Commons does not have a "Report Broken Link" feature, although it is possible to click on the general "Feedback" link to report one.

Searchability   The clean interface design along with the options to browse and use advanced search tools make the search process straightforward and efficient. Like MERLOT, in OER Commons you can start a basic search by typing keywords into the search box in the middle of the webpage or browse by selecting a subject area.

Browsing   You can immediately access the browse function on the main page or click on the "Browse All" button located at the top left portion of the page. This is designed to be easy to use and to provide you with a large subset of results (click here to view the Browsing OER Commons video; http://infogr.am /OER-Commons-Browsing-the-Collection/). It does this by having only one level of category headings and no subheadings. This is a significant limitation because there is no way to narrow down results by topic or related subheadings.

Consequently, the precision of this browsing method is somewhat restricted. Also, there is no browse path because there are not enough subcategories to justify its use. You can gain additional precision refining your search by utilizing the tool bar on the left side of the results page. This will allow you to narrow your results by specifying additional criteria including material type and media format.

You can also begin browsing by grade level and the content partner or provider. If you choose to browse by grade level you can select only primary, secondary, and postsecondary. This does not allow you to narrow resources down to a specific grade, so you can get as many as approximately eight thousand items to begin your browsing. By browsing by libraries and collections, you will need to be knowledgeable about the types of materials they have. Also, some partners have a lot of content and others very little. The browse collection function of the OER Commons is best suited for gaining a better idea of the depth and breadth of the OER collection. It is not the quickest or most precise method of searching.

Basic Search   The basic search of the OER Commons is the quickest method to locating an ILM you are looking for when you have clearly defined keywords. This method is not focused on precision as much as returning all possible results. This means you should get a large number of results including some that are not what you are looking for. For example, a keyword search using "team building" brings up in the results list "Murals: Heritage on the Walls," which does not directly relate to resources for building teams.

You can sort how your results are displayed: by title, relevance, rating, date, and visits. The date function is somewhat limited because you cannot see what the date for the ILM is unless the item itself lists when it was created or copyrighted. Therefore, this function most likely orders items from newest to oldest with regards to when the items were added to the collection.

Quick Tip: Like MERLOT, the OER search box automatically treats multiple keywords with the AND (i.e., +) search operator. OER uses the plus (+) symbol for AND and the minus (–) for NOT. OER uses the exact text search string; therefore, searching "teamwork" will be treated different from searching "team work"; the latter will return more results.

Identical to the browse function, you can refine your results by using the toolbar on the left side of the results page (click here to view the Searching OER Commons video; http://infogr.am/OER-Commons-Basic-Search-Searching-the-Collection/). This allows you to narrow down your returned results by the subject area, grade level, material type, media format, and conditions of use. The material type does not explicitly limit results to tutorials. You can type "tutorial" into the keyword search as an additional search term, but you risk missing results that are relevant if the item does not use the term in its title or description.

Advanced Search   The advanced search tool interface is clean and easy to use. It will take a little more effort, but it allows you to get the most precise results of the search tool options. You can access the Advanced Search tool from the main webpage by clicking on the Advanced Search button. This allows you to search several keyword search options: match all words, the exact phrase, at least one (OR operator), and exclude.

Quick Tip: *To increase the likelihood of finding ILMs, the material type and media format are two of the most useful criteria to use in your search. By using material type you can identify only game and simulations related to your keyword search. You can also attempt to identify tutorials by directly limiting your search using the media format option and select the interactive category.*

Additionally, to increase the precision of your search you can select various criteria such as the language, subject area, material type, course-related materials, member activity, grade level, media format, libraries and collections, conditions of use, OER community type, and OER community topic (click here to view the Advanced Searching OER Commons video; http://infogr.am/OER-Commons-Advanced-Search-Searching-the-Collection/).

The Final Verdict   The OER Commons is one of the largest and fastest growing repositories with international open educational resources including ILMs. It is easy to search and contains high-quality materials. It also has partnerships with a number of content providers that develop ILMs, making it one of the best places to start your search. Table 4.6 shows OER Common's strengths and weaknesses.

Table 4.6
OER Commons Evaluation Scorecard

Five Criteria	Rating (1 Low—5 High)
Collection	★★★★
Validity	★★★★
Significance/Coverage	★★★★★
Design	★★★★
Engagement	★★★
Searchability	★★★
Browsing	★★★
Searching	★★★★
Usability	★★★
Currency	★★
Reliability	★★★★
Overall Score	★★★★

Going Further: Recommended Reading

Monge, S., Ovelar, R., and Azpeitia, I. "Repository 2.0: Social Dynamics to Support Community Building in Learning Object Repositories." *Interdisciplinary Journal of E-Learning and Learning Objects*, 2008, 4, 191–204.

EUROPE
ARIADNE

ARIADNE (http://ariadne.cs.kuleuven.be/AriadneFinder/) is a European foundation created in 1996 by the European Commission's Telematics for Education and Training Program. Today, it is the largest world repository (a massive collection of collections) containing in excess of 600,000 digital learning resources with more than 800,000 searchable through its associated federation of providers (Table 4.7). It is a member of the Global Learning Objects Brokered Exchange (GLOBE — http://www.globe-info.org/index.php) consortium, which is the largest worldwide federation bringing together content from more than seventy

Table 4.7
ARIADNE Features Overview Chart

Subject Areas	All disciplines
Collection Size	800,000+
Collection Type	29 types including games and simulations
Collection Nature	Metasearch referatory
Access (free/fee membership)	Free/institutional membership
Editorial/Review	Not applicable

learning object repositories provided by over fifty organizations. Unlike the previous repositories, an individual membership is not available.

The Collection (Quality, Usability, Currency, and Reliability) The ARI-ADNE site is very basic. It does not provide detailed information about its European members, but it is safe to assume that since membership is limited to educational organizations the quality of the learning materials should be fairly high. It has nearly a million learning resources that can be searched from its site and contains materials for students in K–12 and higher education.

The records of the ARIADNE collections are very barebones, giving only the title, brief description, and keywords. No material quality ratings are given, and no date information is provided beyond what may exist in the title or brief description of the material.

ARIADNE contains nearly ninety different types of materials; they vary in quality more widely than those in the previously examined repositories. Like other repositories that are referatories, its collections only refer (link) to the materials. The currency of the material is difficult to determine from the records unless an item itself has a copyright date.

The reliability of ARIADNE's links is a significant issue for this repository. For example, its website states, "Not all content may be available yet." During the review and testing of the repository, many links to items were broken or not working. Unfortunately, this site does not have a "Report Broken Link" feature.

Searchability Bigger is not always better, and that applies to this repository. While the search design is very simple and easy to use, it is very limited and offers no easy method for browsing. There is only one search option that you can access on the site. You can do this by clicking on the "Try the new Finder now!"

Browsing There is no specific browsing tool in the ARIADNE repository. It is possible to browse the collection using the Finder search tool and selecting one of the following: provider, type, context, format, and language (click here to view the Browsing ARIADNE video; http://infogr.am/ARIADNE-Browsing-the-Collection/). Because there are no subject or discipline categories, the ability to browse the collection is greatly compromised. Additionally, if you select one of the eight providers listed you have to browse through a minimum of 1,700 results, making it very unlikely anyone would be willing to take the time necessary to do this.

Quick Tip: *It is possible to use the type of learning materials to narrow down your browsing results. ARIADNE lists nearly three hundred different types of learning technologies (e.g., videos, Adobe Flash, audio). This can be very handy if you are looking for a specific type of technology.*

It is also possible to browse through any of the nearly ninety types of learning materials but not by subject discipline or category, so finding an object type that is relevant to your course is hit or miss. For example, there are 360 games listed, but all of them originate from the OER Commons. The search tools for the OER Commons are much better, and it makes more sense to simply go to that collection to find the appropriate ILM. There are nearly 2,500 simulations, only about 300 of which come directly from ARIADNE. Even with so few simulations, it is not practical to browse the collection because of the time it would require to possibly find a relevant ILM.

Basic Search The Finder tool is the only searching option available in this repository. It allows you to perform a simple keyword search using a textbox located at the top of the webpage. It is not possible to sort your results.

Typing multiple keywords into the Finder search box will return results that have both the terms entered (i.e., +/AND search operator). The repository does not provide any information on any search operators, and it appears that there is no way for you to use them in the search process. By using the search limiters on the left side of the Finder search page, it is possible to narrow down results by provider, type, context, format, and language (click here to view the Searching ARIADNE video; http://infogr.am/ARIADNE-Basic-Search-Searching-the-Collection/). This function works best when you know what type and format of ILM you are interested in. Simply click on the material type, and this will provide you with a subset of the initial search. For example, a search of "teamwork" returns over five hundred results and about thirty different material types. By selecting games you will return the only result in that type.

Advanced Search   ARIADNE does not currently offer an advanced search function.

The Final Verdict   ARIADNE offers a very basic and simple-to-use search that allows very little customization. Its search technology offers few options to increase the precision of your searches. It is the 900-pound gorilla of repositories in collection size, which gives you access to more international ILMs than any other source. However, this is not the best place to start your search for ILMs; rather, it is a good alternative source when you are struggling to find relevant sources and need to expand your search or if you are looking for a specific technical format for the ILM. Table 4.8 indicates ARIADNE's strengths and weaknesses.

Table 4.8
ARIADNE Evaluation Scorecard

Five Criteria	Rating (1 Low—5 High)
Collection	★★★★
Validity	★★★
Significance/Coverage	★★★★★
Design	★★★
Engagement	★★★
Searchability	★★★★
Browsing	★★★
Searching	★★
Usability	★★★★
Currency	★★★
Reliability	★★★
Overall Score	★★★

Going Further: Recommended Reading

Duval, E., Forte, E., Cardinaels, K., Verhoeven, B., Durm, R. V., Hendrikx, K., Forte, M., Ebel, N., Macowicz, M., Warkentyne, K., and Haenni, F. "DLs for Learning and Global Cooperation—The Ariadne Knowledge Pool System." *Communications of the ACM*, 2001, 44(5), 72–78.

UNITED KINGDOM

JORUM

The JORUM repository (http://www.jorum.ac.uk/) was launched in 2006 and is funded by the United Kingdom's Joint Information Systems Committee (JISC) to be a national repository of teaching materials. It is made up of a coalition of U.K. Higher and Further Education Institutions and provides free access to some of the nearly 18,000 learning and teaching resources (Table 4.9). However, only

Table 4.9
JORUM Features Overview Chart

Subject Areas	37 disciplines (e.g., arts, sciences, math, humanities)
Collection Size	18,000+
Collection Type	All types including games and simulations
Collection Nature	Metasearch referatory
Access (free/fee membership)	Free/institutional membership
Editorial/Review	Peer reviewed

the U.K. Higher and Further Education Institutional members are permitted to submit, download, and have unrestricted access to all materials.

The Collection (Quality, Usability, Currency, and Reliability) The JORUM site is very well designed and easy to use. It provides detailed information about the U.K. institutions that make up the membership, which is limited to educational organizations. There is a peer review process to ensure that the quality of the learning materials is high. Fewer than 20,000 learning resources can be searched from its site, and these are primarily geared toward continuing and higher education students. Though it is one of the smallest of the general repositories, JORUM contains its own unique collection.

The JORUM cataloged records are very detailed and provide the title, author, brief description, keywords, date, and licensing information. However, unlike MERLOT and OER Commons, it does not rate the quality of the material. It does allow you to share the record information through e-mail, Facebook, Twitter, and several other services.

JORUM contains all types of content, and as with other repositories the design of the materials varies in quality more widely than does the content. JORUM, unlike the previously examined repositories, not only links to the materials but also houses them. The currency of its material is easy to determine from the record date added to the repository but may differ from the copyright date of the material itself.

Because this repository houses most of its resources, it has direct control over their accessibility so the links are very reliable. During the review and testing of the repository, no links to items were broken.

Searchability   JORUM's general searchability is good. It has clear and easy-to-use browse, basic, and advanced search capabilities. You can access the browse function by clicking on the "Find" link at the top left side of the website. You can perform a simple keyword search by using the textbox located in the top right corner of the site. To access the advanced search, you must click on the link "Find."

Browsing   JORUM's browsing function is fairly good. From the Find page, you can browse by subject, issue date, author, title, and keyword (click here to view the Browsing JORUM video; http://infogr.am/JORUM-Browsing-the-Collection/). Unless you know a specific author or title, neither is the best option to start browsing the collection. Also, searching by date added is not very practical except to see what was recently added to the collection. The best place to start your browsing is with the subject categories. There are about twenty subjects under HE (higher education) and over thirty under FE (finishing/continuing education).

Quick Tip: A helpful "You are here:" function helps you remember what part of the collection you are searching: for example, "Resources Home » HE » HE — Mathematical and Computer Sciences » Search.

There is only one level of subject browsing, and many of the categories have several hundred resources. This is a serious constraint to browsing JORUM because it is not practical to browse from the first level without first refining your results. You can filter your results by titles, authors, or dates or using keywords. As previously explained, the use of title, author, or date is generally not the best approach. Accordingly, use keywords to refine your search. This limits your ability to navigate through the collection but will help increase the precision of your anticipated results. Another significant limitation of the browse function is that it does not let you automatically limit your search to only open-access resources. Hence, non-members will return many results that are not available to them.

Basic Search The basic search tool works well, but nonmembers should remember to select the radio button for open resources above the search textbox; otherwise, many of the retrieved search results will not be accessible for viewing. The basic search returns results within the advanced search page (click here to view the Searching JORUM video; http://infogr.am/JORUM-Basic-Search-Searching-the-Collection/). This is helpful for refining future results and seeing the criteria applied to your search. JORUM uses the basic search operators (i.e., +, −, and ""), making it easy and convenient to use these functions while conducting a basic search.

JORUM provides you the capability to choose several criteria that will change how your results are displayed. You can select how many results as well as the order in which they are displayed on the page. Additionally, you can sort by relevance, title, issue date, and submit date. The default setting is relevance, but sorting by issue date can be important, especially for fields where information and content can become quickly outdated. The results page also displays your exact search query.

Advanced Search The advanced search function is easy to use and allows you to refine your search (click here to view the Advanced Searching JORUM video; http://infogr.am/JORUM-Advanced-Search-Searching-the-Collection/). However, it does not allow you to refine your search by media type. This is a big disadvantage when compared with MERLOT or OER Commons because it means you will most likely have to view each record of your results to determine what type of ILM it is. It will take you more time to find a specific type of ILM, too. Also, there is no simple radio button to limit results to open resources as there is with using the quick search box. JORUM's advanced search page allows your search to be filtered by full text, title, description, keyword, author, and license.

Quick Tip: Start with the browse function to limit your results to a predefined group (FE or HE) and the associated subject. Then use the advanced search function to narrow down your results.

Table 4.10
JORUM Evaluation Scorecard

Five Criteria	Rating (1 Low—5 High)
Collection	★★★★★
Validity	★★★★
Significance/Coverage	★★★
Design	★★★★
Engagement	★★★★
Searchability	★★★★
Browsing	★★★★
Searching	★★★★
Usability	★★★
Currency	★★★★
Reliability	★★★★★
Overall Score	★★★★

If you are looking for a specific type of ILM, you can use the full text, description, or keyword to try to increase the precision of your search. The full text would likely produce the least specific results but would also include some inaccurate materials, whereas the keyword would return the most specific results but would possibly also leave out some very appropriate materials.

The Final Verdict JORUM offers high-quality international ILMs that are not accessible through other repositories. It also has a pleasant search interface with easy-to-use browse and advanced search tools. However, JORUM possesses several limitations that make it more challenging to search for ILMs. It is one of the smallest repositories and serves as a better secondary repository than a primary one. Table 4.10 indicates JORUM's strengths and weaknesses.

THE FUTURE OF OER REPOSITORIES AND DIGITAL LIBRARIES

The rise of the significance of OER resources for both instructors and students is unquestionable. However, it is unclear how permanent these resources and the sites that make them searchable and accessible will be. It is important that these types of resources be archived for future generations to assure access to high-quality educational resources no matter how technology evolves and changes. Will traditional public and academic libraries become involved with archiving and storing these valuable resources?

This provides a wonderful opportunity for librarians at academic institutions around the world. These professionals must work with faculty, information technologists, and administrators to integrate ILMs into their existing library collections and ensure that institutional ILMs are not lost and are freely accessible to their faculty and students.

The Learning Object Repository Network (LORN) in Australia illustrates this problem and its challenges. Developed through the LORN Business Activity of the Australian Flexible Learning Framework, it is a gateway for digital learning materials from a coalition of several Australian organizations. It has been in existence since the mid-2000s and housed approximately three thousand items. Because of funding issues, LORN was recently discontinued. This now makes accessing the thousands of high-quality educational resources it provided access to much more difficult.

LORN is not the only casualty of loss of funding. LORNET (Learning Object Repositories NETwork) was a Canadian government-funded project that made OERs available; it was discontinued because of funding issues. In this case, the materials were archived and made available through searching MERLOT's "Search Other Libraries" site.

The Educators

Searching College and University Educational Repositories

If I have seen further it is by standing on the shoulders of giants.

— Isaac Newton

Who knows what resources students need better than their instructors? Faculty and support staffs at universities and colleges around the world have been creating interactive learning materials (ILMs) for over a decade. Some universities and colleges have developed high-quality digital repositories and libraries to house all these online learning materials that their faculty are creating, and educators around the world can use most of these for free. This chapter begins by examining some of the very best sources for finding these high-quality, interactive, online educational resources and concludes by explaining how you can also use the general website search tools provided by universities and colleges to directly search for ILMs that faculty and staff have developed at their respective institutions.

This chapter reviews the best college and university digital educational repositories and libraries in detail, including their strengths and weaknesses, and provides detailed descriptions of how to most effectively and efficiently search them. Like the previous chapter, links to an ILM clearinghouse website are included that will have timely, updated short instructional videos with directions on the best search strategies and techniques to use for each of the sources covered in this chapter.

SEARCH STRATEGY POINTS

The best place to start a search for ILMs after trying the large nonprofit repositories like MERLOT and OER Commons is with a college or university institution or consortium repository (Table 5.1). These repositories typically contain only a few ILMs, but they are often excellent.

Table 5.1
Video List for Searching College and University Nonprofit Educational Repositories/Libraries

	Video URL
WISC-ONLINE: Browsing	http://infogr.am/WISC-ONLINE-Browsing-the-Collection/
WISC-ONLINE: Searching	http://infogr.am/WISC-ONLINE-Searching-the-Collection/
NCLOR: Browsing	http://infogr.am/NCLOR-Browsing-the-Collection/
NCLOR: Basic Searching	http://infogr.am/NCLOR-Basic-Search-Searching-the-Collection/
NCLOR: Advanced Searching	http://infogr.am/NCLOR-Advanced-Search-Searching-the-Collection/
KLD: Browsing	http://infogr.am/KLD-Browsing-the-Collection/
KLD: Basic Searching	http://infogr.am/KLD-Basic-Search-Searching-the-Collection/
KLD: Advanced Searching	http://infogr.am/KLD-Advanced-Search-Searching-the-Collection/

Because these sites' collections are smaller, it is advantageous to start with their browse search function. This approach works well because you do not have a large number of resources to sift through. Additionally, you will likely maximize the number of ILMs that match what you are searching for.

Searching an institution's website for ILMs by using either the institution's search tool or a general search engine can be a good alternative for locating existing ILMs. This option is more time-consuming but can uncover high-caliber resources that cannot be discovered in a repository. The key is to identify an institution that has the resources and is known for its expertise in the area in which you are searching.

Locating relevant open courses to find appropriate ILMs is generally a good last resort because the vast majority of course materials made available in these courses does not meet the definition of interactive learning materials.

WISC-ONLINE

Wisc-Online (http://www.wisc-online.com/) was created over a decade ago by a consortium of the sixteen two-year Wisconsin Technical Colleges that received funding from the Fund for the Improvement of Postsecondary Education and the Learning Anytime Anywhere Partnerships as well as the National Science Foundation Advanced Technological Education program. This digital library of Web-based learning resources has a collection of several thousand materials. The collaborative effort to gather materials for the site allows Wisc-Online to have a high level of stability and reliability, which many other institutional digital repositories lack. Table 5.2 provides a list of Wisc-Online's key features. Creating a free account is not required to search and link to ILMs in Wisc-Online but will allow you to benefit from features such as a "My Favorite Objects" Library as well as repository recommendations.

The Collection (Quality, Usability, Currency, and Reliability)

The Wisc-Online website is nicely designed and simple to navigate and use. At fewer than three thousand items, the collection is still small compared with MERLOT and OER Commons. Unlike MERLOT and OER Commons, most of Wisc-Online's available materials are some type of ILM, which makes it one of the larger online ILM repositories. Additionally, these materials are not likely to be found in any other online repository. Because all the materials are developed by

Table 5.2
Wisc-Online Features Overview

Subject Areas	ABE/ELL, business, general education, health, professional development, service, and technical
Collection Size	2,300+
Collection Type	Most items are ILMs: tutorials, animations, and games
Collection Nature	Repository
Access (free/fee membership)	Free individual membership
Editorial/Review	Approved by development faculty and staff

a team of developers and the content for the ILMs is provided by faculty experts, the overall quality is quite good. Additionally, to promote the best materials the site allows everyone to rate the item or comment on it.

The records displayed after browsing the collection provide only the title and brief description of the material. The site does allow you to click to go right to the material that also displays the author of the content. Surprisingly there is no detailed record that gives any additional information such as item creation date, although some of the items have copyright dates. The records displayed after conducting a keyword search contain author and rating information in addition to the title and brief description.

Wisc-Online is a true repository housing the materials in its library. This is a great strength because it means you will generally not find any broken links to the items themselves. The currency of the material is not easy to determine, which poses a potential problem as items age.

Searchability

The Wisc-Online repository has a functional and simple search interface using clear browsing and a basic keyword search textbox tool. You can access the browse function by clicking on the "Learning Objects" link located on the right-hand side of the top navigation bar of the website. You can perform a very basic keyword search by using the textbox located in the top right corner of the website. There is no advanced search feature, which is a distinct disadvantage to users' ability to conduct a precise keyword search.

Browsing

Wisc-Online's browsing function works quite well, and because of the small size of the repository it is the best way to start your search (click here to view the Browsing Wisc-Online video; http://infogr.am/WISC-ONLINE-Browsing-the-Collection/). From the "Learning Objects" page, you can browse by subject heading via two levels. This makes it quick and easy to get to a list of related items under the categories, which often will have only several dozen items.

> *Quick Tip*: *Because Wisc-Online does not offer an advanced search tool, the best method for locating appropriate ILMs is to use the browse function. This will ensure that you do not find irrelevant results and also that you don't miss appropriate ones.*

There are no additional ways for you to refine your results. This is not a significant disadvantage because of the limited number of materials in the repository. Surprisingly, you cannot see how many resources are under each criterion as you browse.

Keyword Search

The keyword search tool is very basic and is not designed to use search operators like AND or NOT. The search tool automatically uses the OR operator between multiple words, which means you will get all the results containing either word in your results (click here to view the Searching Wisc-Online video; http://infogr.am/WISC-ONLINE-Searching-the-Collection/). This is not ideal if you are seeking precise results because you will often get items that are not appropriate. For example, performing a search using the words "team building" will return results with the word "building" in it but not "team." Therefore, if you are looking for something on the topic of working with teams, you may get a result like "building a resume" because it contains the word "building" in it.

Wisc-Online does give you the ability to refine your results by selecting a relevant subject heading, and it lists how many items are in each category. The default setting for displaying results is by relevance, and there is no way to sort your results list in the repository. The results page does display your exact search query, and by clicking on the "View" link you can go right to the item.

Final Verdict

Wisc-Online is a relative small, high-quality repository offering ILMs that are not accessible through any other repository. The browse function works fairly well, but the search tool is rudimentary. However, the small size of the repository helps it to overcome its search flaws by making it easy to browse and search the collection. Despite not offering an advanced full-text search tool that uses AND, OR, or NOT, it is a good choice to use because it contains excellent ILMs. Table 5.3 indicates Wisc-Online's strengths and weaknesses.

Table 5.3
Wisc-Online Evaluation Scorecard

Five Criteria	Rating (1 Low – 5 High)
Collection	★★★★
Validity	★★★★★
Significance/Coverage	★★★
Design	★★★★★
Engagement	★★★★★
Searchability	★★★★
Browsing	★★★★★
Searching	★★★
Usability	★★★★★
Currency	★★★★★
Reliability	★★★★★
Overall Score	★★★★★

Going Further: Recommended Readings

Polsani, P. "Use and Abuse of Reusable Learning Objects." *Journal of Digital Information*, 2003, 3(4). http://journals.tdl.org/jodi/article/view/89.

NCLOR

The North Carolina Learning Object Repository (NCLOR; http://explorethelor .org/) was established in 2006 in a joint effort by the North Carolina Community College System (composed of fifty-eight public community colleges in North Carolina), University of North Carolina (UNC) System, North Carolina Independent Colleges and Universities (composed of thirty-six private institutions), the North Carolina Department of Public Instruction (DPI), and North Carolina Virtual Public School (NCVPS). It was designed to be the central gateway for all teachers from prekindergarten to college graduate level in the state to access, collect, share, and contribute high-quality digital learning resources. It is a fairly large repository, containing nearly 10,000 resources. While the NCLOR was developed for educators in North Carolina and provides them the ability to register for an account, it is possible to log on as a guest to search. The software platform that NCLOR is built on is Pearson's commercial learning object repository EQUELLA. Table 5.4 provides a list of NCLOR's key features.

Table 5.4
NCLOR Features Overview

Subject Areas	Most disciplines (e.g., sciences, math, humanities)
Collection Size	10,000+
Collection Type	All types including simulations, games, and tutorials
Collection Nature	Metasearch referatory
Access (free/fee membership)	Free/North Carolina and guest membership
Editorial/Review	Peer reviewed

The Collection (Quality, Usability, Currency, and Reliability)

The site, redesigned on November 30, 2011, is well designed and does a good job of being both functional and user-friendly. Many of its 10,000 resources can be found in other repositories and online libraries. The overall quality of the materials included in the NCLOR library is quite good; it includes a space for ratings and comment fields, but many of the materials are not rated.

Like many other repositories, NCLOR contains two types of records. The basic record is displayed after conducting a search or browsing the collection. It gives very basic information like title and description. However, unlike other repositories you cannot click to preview the material but have to click on the title to go to the detailed record. The full record provides additional information about the description of use, learning resource type, discipline, keywords, and technical requirements.

Like its counterparts, NCLOR contains many types of content including several thousand tutorials, several hundred simulations, and more than sixty games. The currency of the material is not always easy to determine, but a "Last Updated" field shows how recently the record has been modified. The reliability of the links for this repository appears to be very good, and no broken links were observed during the review and evaluation of this repository.

Searchability

NCLOR includes a dashboard, and its layout and design make its general searchability good. The browse, quick, and preformatted advanced search options are simple to use. You can access the browse function directly from the dashboard by clicking on one of the four "Browse" link options located on the left navigation bar of the website. You can perform a simple keyword search by using the textbox located in the top center of the "Search" webpage. The preformatted advanced search option can be accessed by clicking on the "Search" link located near the top of the left navigation bar of the website.

Browsing

The NCLOR browsing function is quite beneficial, especially if you want to gain a better understanding of what subjects or learning resource types are available from the repository. From the dashboard, you can browse by discipline, learning resource type, education level, and resource series (i.e., the origin of the materials). There are two levels of discipline (subject) browsing results (click here to view the

Browsing NCLOR video; http://infogr.am/NCLOR-Browsing-the-Collection/).
Additionally, there are less than two dozen categories to select from, many of
them containing only a few hundred resources. This, combined with the ability to
refine your initial browsing results with a filter tool, makes it easy to customize a
more precise list of materials.

*Quick Tip: The quickest way to find ILMs in NCLOR is to start your brows-
ing with the "Learning Resource Type" option and then selecting "Game,"
"Simulation," or "Tutorial." Once you do this, use the keyword filter tool to
display only discipline-specific results.*

You can refine your results by using a filter toolbox that displays after you select
an initial browse type. The filter gives you the ability to limit your results by keywords, date, and resource type. The resource type can be useful when you want to
quickly identify a resource's multimedia elements. However, since NCLOR does
allow you to browse by learning resource type, which includes games, tutorials,
and simulations, you should consider starting with this browse function if you
want to go right to a certain type of material.

As you browse you can see how many resources are under each criterion.
Another helpful tool is that you can choose how to sort your results. The default
is set to relevance, but you can also choose date (record was last modified), title
(alphabetical), and user rating (highest to lowest). The user rating option will not
be very useful until the number of items rated drastically increases.

Basic Search

The quick search tool is very simple and works fine, but it was originally
designed to use search operators like AND, OR, and NOT (click here to view
the Searching NCLOR video; http://infogr.am/NCLOR-Basic-Search-Searching-
the-Collection/). The quick search is designed to search the metadata of the
records and then return results based on the title, description, and keywords. The
returned search results highlight the search word in the returned item records
and can be sorted just like the browsable results. The quick search allows you to
filter your initial quick search query only by date or resource type and not by
additional keywords.

Advanced Search

The advanced search function offers several preset options and is different from any other reviewed repository. You have to first type in a keyword search and then select from the following methods of advanced search you want to perform from within a drop-down menu box: discipline/level, learning resource type, NCCCS Student Learning Outcomes, and nursing content results (click here to view the Advanced Searching NCLOR video; http://infogr.am/NCLOR-Advanced-Search-Searching-the-Collection/).

Quick Tip: *To get the most out of the advanced search tool, use the limiter "Learning Resource Type" so that you can search only for ILMs.*

Once you have selected the sort of advanced search you want to employ, you must then click on the "Edit Query" link directly under the "Within" menu drop-down box, and you are immediately transferred to a new page with checkboxes that allow you to select which additional search criteria you want to use to narrow down your search results. This makes the advanced search option much less user-friendly than the alternatives. Fortunately, the most recent updated version of the NCLOR advanced search does allow you to refine your results using search operators; this is useful when it comes to refining your results and returning the most precise ILMs possible. The advanced search tool does allow you to sort and filter your results just like the browsing and quick search options.

The Final Verdict

North Carolina Learning Object Repository is a smaller, high-quality repository that offers a few ILMs not accessible through other repositories. It also has an expedient quick search tool and a good browse search tool. Its biggest disadvantage, other than its smaller size, is that it does not offer a very robust advanced search tool. This repository is a good choice to augment your search for ILMs because it functions as a meta-repository search tool. However, beyond its intended users—North Carolina educators—NCLOR should be considered a secondary source until it can grow the size of its own unique collection and

Table 5.5
NCLOR Evaluation Scorecard

Five Criteria	Rating (1 Low – 5 High)
Collection	★★★★
Validity	★★★★
Significance/Coverage	★★★
Design	★★★★
Engagement	★★★
Searchability	★★★★
Browsing	★★★★
Searching	★★★★
Usability	★★★★
Currency	★★★★
Reliability	★★★★
Overall Score	★★★★

improve upon the repository's advanced search features. Table 5.5 indicates NCLOR's strengths and weaknesses.

THE KENTUCKY LEARNING DEPOT

The Kentucky Learning Depot (KLD) repository (http://kylearningdepot.org/) is a statewide initiative in Kentucky to store, manage, and provide access to digital educational resources. It was launched at the end of 2009 and is still relatively small. The repository is a joint effort led by the Council on Postsecondary Education and the Kentucky Department of Education. The Kentucky Education Cabinet, Education Professional Standards Board, KET, Kentucky Adult Education, Kentucky Department of Libraries and Archives, and prekindergarten–12 schools and postsecondary institutions are all collaborators on this project. It is designed to be the central gateway for all state kindergarten–20 educators. Currently, membership is available only for Kentucky educators; however, guest access is provided so that anyone can search and access many of the learning

Table 5.6
KLD Features Overview

Subject Areas	18 disciplines including art, math, and sciences
Collection Size	6,000+
Collection Type	All types including tutorials, animations, and games
Collection Nature	Repository
Access (free/fee membership)	Free guest/Kentucky educators
Editorial/Review	Approved by development faculty and staff

resources. Like NCLOR, KLD is built on Pearson's EQUELLA commercial platform (http://www.equella.com/home.php). Table 5.6 provides a list of KLD's key features.

The Collection (Quality, Usability, Currency, and Reliability)

KLD is a well-designed site balancing functionality with accessibility, and it provides access to more than six thousand items. However, the majority of these materials are not for postsecondary education. Some of the items contained in the depot are not currently found in any other repository. Additionally, the overall quality of the materials is quite good. You can also sort the search results by user ratings.

There are two types of records in the repository. The brief record is displayed after conducting a search or browsing the collection. It provides very basic information like title and brief description, date material was added to the collection, the version, and the status, and you can go directly to the material or to a more detailed record. The detailed record provides some additional information such as the educational level, related keywords, technical format, learning resource type, and usage rights. Additionally, because no broken links were observed, the reliability of the links for this repository appears to be strong.

Searchability

KLD's general materials searchability is quite good. It has a clear and very easy-to-use browse, basic, and advanced search. You can access the browse function by clicking on any of the four browsing options located on the left navigation bar of the website once you are logged in as a guest. You can perform a simple keyword search by using the textbox located in the top right corner of the webpage. The advanced search can be accessed by clicking on the link located on the top left corner of the same page.

Browsing

The browsing function of the KLD is very helpful, especially if you want to gain a better understanding of what is largely available from the repository. From the "Browse" page, you can look at the entire collection (not recommended) or view results by collection, discipline, or education level (click here to view the Browsing KLD video; http://infogr.am/KLD-Browsing-the-Collection/). There is only one level of discipline browsing: by subject. Currently, there are only eighteen categories, with many of them containing less than a hundred resources. This combined with the ability to refine your initial results makes it easy to create a browsable list.

Quick Tip: The best place to start your browsing is with the "Discipline" categories. KLD is one of the few repositories containing all three ILM material types.

You can refine your results using all of the aforementioned criteria. However, what once set KLD apart from the crowd was the ability to limit by learning resource type. This is very useful because you can immediately search the exact type of interactive learning material resource you are looking to integrate into your course. However, the recent upgrade changed this option so that now it is accessible only using the "Advanced Search" option. Because the repository currently has a somewhat small number of learning resources for higher education, it is possible to browse very quickly to see if the topic or discipline has a game, simulation, or tutorial. It will become more necessary to use keywords to help refine your browsing results as the number of educational resources for higher education grows.

It is possible to sort the results you get while browsing the collection by popularity, date, title, and user rating. Also helpful is that the site gives you the total number of items in your browsing results. It is also possible for you to choose how many results you want to display while you browse from ten to one hundred.

Basic Search

The basic search tool is straightforward and simple to use (click here to view the Searching KLD video; http://infogr.am/KLD-Basic-Search-Searching-the-Collection/). It is designed to use Boolean search operators such as AND, OR, or NOT as well as search wildcards such as "", *, and ?. The quick search is designed to examine the metadata of the records and then return results based on the relevance. The returned search results show the keyword search criteria highlighted in yellow. Just as when you are browsing, the return results are displayed in brief records and can be sorted and displayed as explained previously. It is also possible with the basic search to further refine your returned results.

Advanced Search

The advanced search function for the most part is simple and easy to use (click here to view the Advanced Searching KLD video; http://infogr.am/KLD-Advanced-Search-Searching-the-Collection/). There are several helpful ways to refine your search: using search operators; selecting limiters such as discipline, education level, and learning resource type; and using a controlled vocabulary of search terms such as the CIP, ERIC, and GEM. However, most people will be unfamiliar with these terms and will not find this function very useful.

Quick Tip: To find the most interactive resources, search using the learning resource type and select the kind of ILM you want, such as a game.

The Kentucky Learning Depot's advanced search page allows you to select criteria, in addition to performing a keyword search, and to limit your search results. At the time the site was reviewed, it was having technical issues that prevented the search criteria from limiting the results correctly. Most notably for finding ILMs, it is possible to search by learning resource type.

The Final Verdict

The Kentucky Learning Depot is a very small, high-quality repository offering some ILMs that are not accessible through other repositories. It also has a simple and easy-to-use basic search tool and very functional browse and advanced search tool. Its biggest disadvantage is the size of its ILM collection. This repository is a superb choice to augment your search for ILMs but, like other smaller repositories, should be considered a tertiary repository until its collection size for postsecondary students greatly expands. Table 5.7 indicates KLD's strengths and weaknesses.

TRAILBLAZING IN SEARCH OF HIGHER EDUCATION'S ILM

Colleges and universities around the country (and world) offer a vast amount of mostly untapped excellent interactive educational resources, many of which would be considered interactive learning materials. These resources are online and made freely available to educators and students for educational purposes. The challenge is that most of them have not created a digital repository or library for external

Table 5.7
KLD Evaluation Scorecard

Five Criteria	Rating (1 Low – 5 High)
Collection	★★★
Validity	★★★★★
Significance/Coverage	★★
Design	★★★★
Engagement	★★★
Searchability	★★★★
Browsing	★★★★
Searching	★★★★
Usability	★★★★★
Currency	★★★★
Reliability	★★★★★
Overall Score	★★★★

faculty, librarians, educational support staff, and students. Consequently, it is very difficult and time-consuming for most faculty and students to try to locate these resources themselves.

You can employ some techniques to help increase the speed and precision of your search. The remainder of this chapter focuses on how to search and locate very high-quality ILMs that may not yet be available from an existing online repository or digital library. Like with anything else, the best approach is to start with what you already know: your own institution. You might be surprised by the quality and quantity of what you discover. For example, Penn State University (like most others) is still in the early stages of developing and implementing a repository for learning objects that will include faculty-developed ILMs. This means that if you are looking for a chemistry-related tutorial you have only a couple of options beyond knowing a particular faculty or staff member who may have worked on the creation of an ILM.

You can use either the university's "Find" search tool on the website's main page or a search engine like Google and limit the retrieval to only the psu.edu domain. You will need to determine which choice is best, depending on the search tools and functions the institution provides. In the Penn State example, you can start with the university's basic search tool (which also includes an advanced search function). By typing in "chemistry modules" in the search box, you get over six thousand results — far too many to review and most of which will not be useful. However, you get several good ILMs among the first few results. One of the top results is the Center for Learning & Teaching at Berks. This link leads you to a stoichiometry tutorial.

If you had started with a general search engine like Google and used the advanced search screen to limit the results to only the Penn State domain, you would have also been provided a link to the same stoichiometry tutorial — slightly farther down the results list. The Google advanced search has as its second result "Module Synopsis" (chemistry modules), which is not listed on the first page of the Penn State search results list. Nevertheless, this set of modules does not contain a stoichiometry module. In this example, if you had been interested in finding additional stoichiometry tutorials, games, or simulations, then it would be important to conduct the search again, both with the university's search tool and with the Google advanced search tool, using "chemistry modules" as keywords.

The greatest challenge to finding ILMs developed at colleges and universities (beyond what the aforementioned repositories contain) is that you are faced with a situation that is not unlike looking for a needle in a haystack. There are several thousand higher-education institutions in the United States and many more when you consider all the colleges and universities in English-speaking countries. So how do you go about effectively and efficiently searching for high-quality digital learning materials outside of the sources already examined throughout this book (Figure 5.1)?

The best approach is to first consider the institutions that would most likely have the most resources (faculty and staff), research expertise, and scalability (i.e., large course enrollments) to justify the time and effort it takes to develop good-quality ILMs. This means that large research universities and colleges would be the best candidates to start a search.

This still leaves hundreds of possibilities, so where do you begin? Begin with institutions that have highly ranked programs within the areas or subjects of interest that you are seeking to find a related game, simulation, or module/tutorial. Within your own academic domain, you most likely already have a good idea of which schools have good reputations associated with their degree programs; this is a good starting point.

Nevertheless, sometimes you may be searching for an ILM that is outside your primary domain, and you may need some assistance in identifying appropriate

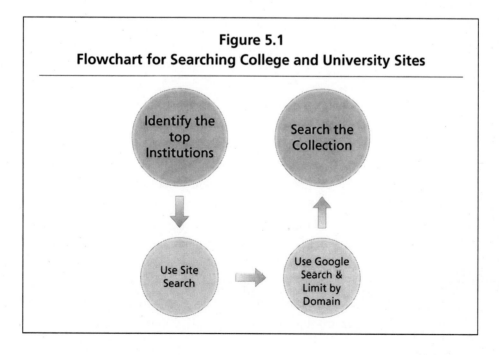

Figure 5.1
Flowchart for Searching College and University Sites

institutions. This is when it is necessary to conduct a simple search online to identify top college and university programs. For example, if you wanted to locate some type of ILM that would be related to the medical field, you could do an online search to discover the top-ranked medical schools. You would—probably unsurprisingly—discover that Harvard Medical School is one of the top-ranked programs in the country. Therefore, this university website might be a good starting point when looking for useful ILMs.

Like in the Penn State University example, you will likely want to use both the general search tool that Harvard makes available on its website and also use a search engine like Google, making sure to limit your results to the appropriate domain harvard.edu. The more specific the terms or words used in your search, usually the more precise your results. If you don't get many results, you will want to broaden and expand your search terms. In the Harvard example, a good general search for a tutorial would be constructed as a keyword search with the following terms "tutorial" and "medical."

Conducting this search with the Harvard University website search tool would give you over a thousand results, but none of the results on the first page would take you to an actual tutorial. Doing the very same search using Google to search the Harvard website would produce even more results: over five thousand. Nevertheless, the first several results take you directly to various medical tutorials. Once you are able to refine your results by choosing a more specific topic, you will want to conduct another search. In this example, the search engine provided better results than the university search tool. You should stick with whichever is returning the most precise results.

Let us consider one other general example demonstrating the effectiveness of university Web search tools. Consider that you are looking to find a simulation that would allow students in an engineering class to explore a concept or principle in physics. Once again, if you have already searched the large general repositories (i.e., MERLOT, OER Commons) and the higher education repositories (i.e., NCLOR, KLD) and found very little useful resources, you will want to figure out what other universities or colleges might be worth your time and effort to search. Assuming you are familiar with only a couple of top engineering schools, you will want to conduct a Web search to identify some of the other top public and private institutions.

By conducting this search (in the United States) you would discover that the engineering program at the University of Colorado at Boulder is highly ranked.

You can either start your search at the school's website or use a search engine. By going to the University of Colorado at Boulder's website and conducting a keyword search using the terms "physics" and "simulations," you would return over 1,700 results, but the very first result would link you to the PhET site (http://phet.colorado.edu). Conducting the very same search using Google gives over 15,000 results, although the first few links in the results list take you to the same PhET site.

PhET includes hundreds of interactive simulations. By simply clicking on "Play with Sims," you are taken to a page that allows you to browse the simulation by topic or grade level and to conduct a simple keyword search to find a specific type of simulation. By clicking on the physics link you are taken directly to over eighty simulations under that classification.

Google powers the search tool from University of Colorado at Boulder; you can use an advanced search tool page that gives additional criteria to help narrow down your results. It also provides search tips and an automatically generated list of related terms that allow you to narrow down your search results. There is no absolute certainty that by using an institution's Web search tool you will be able to find the ILMs developed by faculty and staff; therefore, it is important to also use a general search engine to conduct that same type of search.

EMERGING TRENDS AND SEARCH TOOLS IN HIGHER EDUCATION

Around the turn of the century, colleges and universities began experimenting with making entire courses and their related materials available for free via the Internet. These open courseware initiatives have gained momentum over the past decade. A number of prestigious institutions now offer courses and the associated lectures and resources: MIT, Harvard, University of California at Berkeley, Wellesley, Georgetown University, Michigan State University, University of Michigan, University of Pennsylvania, California Institute of Technology, Arizona State University, and Notre Dame University. To learn more about these institutions and discover other higher education institutions making courses freely available, visit the OpenCourseWare (OCW) Consortium (http://www.ocwconsortium.org/). Most recently, startup companies like Udacity, Coursera, and EDx have launched their own massive online open courses (MOOCs), but these sites cannot be easily searched for ILM content. In the future the courses will probably have ILMs embedded in them.

This would seem to be an excellent place to find ILMs. Currently, this is not the case because the vast majority of content made accessible via open courseware initiatives does not meet the definition of interactive learning materials. Most of these courses offer only syllabi, lecture notes, assignments, and class materials in audio and video format. These resources can be very useful but are not designed to engage students the way that ILMs are.

However, if you are not able to locate ILMs through the better options already explored in this book (e.g., MERLOT, OER Commons, Wisc-Online), it is worth considering searching these courses. Similar to using a Web search engine, first identify the institutions that have the best programs and courses in the discipline in which you would like to find the ILM. Then cross-reference this with the institutions' participation in an open courseware initiative. Once you locate several potential courses offered by various colleges and universities, then explore the materials that each of these courses makes freely available. Unfortunately, this approach is very time-consuming because you have to browse the course activities and resources one by one.

Another emerging trend is the use of social media such as Twitter and Facebook by faculty as learning tools in their courses. While these social network platforms will not likely house ILMs, they may become increasingly useful in locating those that faculty use in their courses. For example, by conducting a Twitter search and using the same approaches discussed earlier in this chapter, with Web search engines you may be able to identify an ILM that you would not have discovered through Google or Bing.

The aforementioned trends, along with the development of personal learning networks and the rise of digital citizen curators who use tools such as Scoop.it and Pinterest, will lead to new modes for discovering interactive learning materials. These combined with emerging technology might one day become the preferred method for locating ILMs, but presently the best resources remain the digital repositories and libraries that institutions are developing for their faculty and students.

GOING FURTHER: ADDITIONAL EDUCATIONAL REPOSITORIES

Rice University, "Connexions," http://cnx.org/
This repository is not explicitly designed to share ILMs. It was started at Rice University in 1999 and houses open educational resources primarily made up of textbooks, lessons, learning materials, and scholarly works geared toward K–12 students. Subject areas

include computer science, math, and music. A growing number of ILMs are embedded in its educational modules and can be used by higher education students and faculty. To learn more about the resource visit http://blog.chron.com/computingatrice/2010/04/a-little-bit-about-connexions/ and http://thetechawards.thetech.org/the-laureates/stories/1423.

National Digital Learning Resources Initiative, "NDLR," https://dspace.ndlr.ie/jspui/

This repository of digital learning content is a joint venture of seven universities in Ireland, the Dublin Institute of Technology, and thirteen Institutes of Technology. The repository is fairly large, with more than 27,000 resources. It is a freely available, open, online community primarily intended for faculty of higher education in Ireland but can be used by educators and students worldwide. It does contain some ILMs and is a well-designed repository with basic browse and search capabilities.

EDx, https://www.edx.org/

This open courseware initiative launched in 2012 with a partnership between Harvard and MIT and has been adding other colleges and universities to its platform. Currently, it does not have a robust course offering from other institutions, but this could change quickly as more than two hundred higher educational institutions have shown interest in partnering in this endeavor. The courses and site are not specifically designed to find and share ILMs. However, as the number of courses offered grows and as faculty look to create more engagement for online learners it is quite likely that ILMs will increasingly be embedded in the course materials and accessed freely to educators and students around the world.

The Entrepreneurs

Textbook Publishers, Entertainment Media, and Educational Software Companies

The confluence of digital computing technologies that is occurring today is driving the creation of a new educational market for digital learning materials. Up to this point, this book has focused on not-for-profit educational organizations and institutions that have been developing, sharing, or disseminating interactive learning materials (ILMs) for educators. Increasingly, for-profit companies are realizing that there is a nascent educational market for ILMs.

The biggest players in this newly emerging market are textbook publishers, educational entertainment media, and educational computer software companies (Table 6.1). This chapter focuses on how instructors, librarians, and instructional technologists can go about finding and using these for-profit companies' interactive educational resources. Unlike the materials available from nonprofits, it costs money to use many of the ILMs discussed here. However, some materials do not need to be purchased and are free to use for educational purposes.

The structure of this chapter is different from the last couple. In the current environment there is no agreed upon general and consistent means by which to share or circulate interactive digital educational resources. This creates a situation that makes it very challenging to find these interactive, educational resources

Table 6.1

Video List for Searching Textbook Publishers, Entertainment Media, and Educational Software Companies

	Video URL
PBS: Browsing	http://infogr.am/PBS-Browsing-the-Collection/
PBS Teachers: Browsing	http://infogr.am/PBS-Teachers-Browsing-the-Collection/
iTunes: Searching	http://infogr.am/iTUNES-Searching/

because each organization approaches how they catalog and share these resources differently. There are several tips to keep in mind as you read through the chapter.

Textbook publishers and entertainment media link their ILMs to the textbooks and programming, respectively, that they publish. This means you will need to look up the textbook or program you are interested in and then look on their website to see what related online materials (often labeled "For Teachers") come with the publication or program. Educational software companies often have a library of educational software titles that you can look up. However, Apple's approach with iTunes and its searchable and downloadable marketplace for educational applications is likely to become the standard in the near future.

TEXTBOOK PUBLISHERS

A number of factors influence the development of engaging digital learning materials by large textbook publishers like McGraw-Hill, Pearson, Cengage, and Wiley, including the rising cost of textbooks; new digital printing and dissemination technologies; and the broader adoption of e-readers, notebook, and netbook computing devices. However, the rise of digital learning analytics and assessment tools, in conjunction with the rise of massive online open courses (MOOCs) and the evolution of learning management systems (LMSs) like Blackboard, may increasingly drive the development and adoption of ILMs. Since these types of resources can easily be embedded into an LMS and online courses as well as provide detailed feedback both to the learner and the instructor, they can be viewed as increasingly vital teaching and learning resources.

Publishers are using ILMs as important resources coupled with their existing textbooks. This approach views the ILMs as ancillary or simply digital support resources for textbook products. In the future, the ILMs might be directly embedded into digital textbooks. Then, as students read their textbooks they would encounter all types of interactive multimedia materials in addition to the text itself. Students would be able to immediately click on and experience various types of tutorials, games, and simulations.

This is a very appealing model since faculty could bring these resources right into the classroom and have a dialogue with students about material. Also, learning analytics could be built into the resources so that both the instructor and student could see how they are performing and meeting learning objectives and course outcomes. In the progressively social networked world in which we live, both instructor and student may also increasingly demand that they have greater control in rating and choosing the types of ILMs they embed into their learning experiences (e.g., LMSs, e-books). This type of personalized learning environment (PLE) is already gaining traction in higher education. However, the downside of this type of learning process is that it is often more time-consuming and at times runs afoul of existing copyright law.

You are probably familiar with learning management systems such as Blackboard; most colleges and universities now support at least one of these systems. Increasingly, instructors can also bypass their institution's LMS and select one of the many free proprietary or open-source, instructor-geared options (e.g., CoursSites.com, NineHub.com). Over the past decade, these types of online learning systems have moved from the exception to the rule for how instructors make course content available to students. Publishers are increasingly partnering with or even buying or developing their own LMSs (e.g., Pearson's OpenClass) products so that they can use them as delivery platforms for their content.

Many educational publishers have been developing ancillary materials over the past decade, and increasingly they are working on more interactive and multimedia modules containing tutorials, games, and simulations. The current practice is to make these resources available to both instructors and students. Generally, the course instructor has more access to these types of materials through the publisher's website, which is often password protected and requires instructors to sign up for an account. As an instructor, once you have an account you have access to the host of digital resources that go along with your course textbook, which you can then import into your LMS. These often include ILMs; however, it is up to you to decide what ILMs you want to integrate into your LMS (or Web-enhanced course).

Before adopting a traditional or digital textbook, you may want to spend more time evaluating the types of ILMs that publishers are embedding or enhancing their content with. As with repositories, ILMs' quality and amount can vary widely. Increasingly, more and more textbook publishers are offering quality digital resources with their textbooks.

Publishers are also developing products of their own, in addition to integrating content through an LMS. These new products will make ILMs accessible and embeddable into a faculty member's online course site. The following are examples of leaders in the development and integration of these types of resources.

- **McGraw-Hill's Higher Education division** (http://catalogs.mhhe.com/mhhe/home.do) has a product called Connect that allows instructors to access their content and digital adaptive learning tools. In July 2010, they partnered with Blackboard Inc. to create " ... seamless access to McGraw-Hill Connect to manage course content, create assignments and track student performance. In addition, users will also gain access to a range of popular tools that come with the platform, including adaptive assessment to deliver customized learning content based on student strengths and weaknesses ... " (Blackboard, 2010)

- **Pearson's Higher Education division** (http://www.pearsonlearning solutions.com/online-learning/) has two products that are relevant to ILMs. EQUELLA (http://www.equella.com/home.php) allows institutions to develop their own digital institutional repository for educational resources. Pearson recently released a new version of EQUELLA that " ... provides a central solution to meet an institution's learning, research, media and library needs. Faculty, instructional designers and academic technologists can easily search in one location for all of their learning content — video, custom eBooks, presentations, lecture captures and more — all tagged by metadata such as learning outcomes, grade level and relevant keywords" (Pearson, 2011).

- **Openclass** (http://www.joinopenclass.com/open/view/t1) is Person's new (and free) learning management system. It debuted at EDUCAUSE in October 2011. It remains to be seen how fast this system will be adopted by institutions. If successful, it could be a power tool to enable the sharing of ILMs across institutions.

- **Cengage Learning's Higher Education division** (http://www.cengagesites .com/academic/?site=5232) is designed to work with existing LMSs and let instructors integrate all types of digital resources into their online course. The MindApps system creates " ... learning paths that integrate content and learning activity applications that map directly to an instructor's syllabus or curriculum. Unlike other products which are affiliated with a single Learning Management System (LMS), MindTap is LMS agnostic and designed to work with any supported LMS the instructor chooses to use. Students can navigate through a customized dashboard of readings, assignments, and other course information. This powerful combination of personalized content and on-the-go access encourages interactivity, increases student engagement and improves learning outcomes" (Cengage, 2011).

- **Wiley's Higher Education division** (http://www.wiley.com/WileyCDA /Brand/id-28.html) Wiley Plus (http://www.wiley.com/WileyCDA/Brand/id-31.html?&category=For+Learning) is a course management system that contains an integrated suite of learning and teaching resources. This, like other LMS systems, looks to integrate textbook resources with additional learning materials.

ENTERTAINMENT AND EDUCATIONAL MEDIA

Today's world constantly bombards us with media through many devices— portable televisions, computers, cell phones—that travel with us. We live in a society where we can choose what shows, movies, and videos we watch as well as when we watch them. This dynamic of convenience, combined with technologies that give all of us the availability to develop our own media content, means that we are surrounded by exponentially ever expanding media programming. The current generation expects media to play a role in their educational experience since it is such an integrated part of their daily lives.

Unsurprisingly, companies and organizations that professionally produce media content such as television programs and movies are increasingly seeing the value of creating digital learning materials to enhance their content and draw viewers' interest and engagement with that programming. Not unlike textbook publishers, these organizations see ILMs as materials that can help sell their programming. This means that some of these materials are available at no cost for educators to use in their classes. Many of these media producers thus far have focused on K–12 children, but as students increasingly use ILMs they will come to expect them in higher education, too. Faculty in higher education may find that these resources are quite appropriate for lower-level courses or that they help provide additional remediation to students in college course prerequisites.

Still, only in the past decade have these companies started creating these resources for their programming. This, coupled with the fact that there is no agreed upon general and consistent means by which to share or circulate these types of resources, creates an environment that can make it difficult to find these interactive, educational resources. This section of the chapter examines how you can most effectively and efficiently find these digital resources.

Three primary approaches can be used to find ILMs from these educational media content providers. One method involves identifying a relevant show, movie, or program that relates directly to the topic or content you are looking to find. This means if you are unfamiliar with entertainment or educational media producers' programming, you first must generally identify a likely source to look for relevant ILMs. Once you do this you can then go right to the website and look under their shows or programming content, which is usually accessed by simply finding a link at the top or left navigation bar. Then when you are at a particular television show's website you can look for an additional link to take you to the ILMs developed for that show.

Usually, a show's Web page has a link that might state "Interactive Resources" or "Games and More" or might have a resource section for teachers. This is where you will be able to access any possible ILMs. Quite often sites will display the results in an easy-to-browse format.

To illustrate this process better, the following section will examine some of the best sources with which to start when attempting to find an ILM to integrate into your course. For example, the aforementioned ILM search strategy can be applied to several good sources such as the Discovery Channel (DC), Public Broadcasting Network (PBS), the History Channel, or an international source like the British Broadcasting Corporation (BBC). We will examine both the Discovery Channel and PBS, which both exemplify and typify what you will encounter when using this method to search for ILMs at their sites.

Browsing DC

If you teach a course in meteorology, you might want to find ILMs to help your students when you study tornadoes. You could simply browse DC's programming, or if you know that it has a show called *Storm Chasers* you could go to its home page and select TV shows right from the top navigation bar for the site. Then you can click on the link provided there to go right to the *Storm Chasers* page. This would then give you access to a link called "Games and More." By clicking on this link you would be taken to a section containing extra content including " … games, puzzles, quizzes and interactives … " A list of only about a dozen resources is provided, and some of these games or interactive resources qualify as ILMs.

Quick Tip: This method works best when you are already familiar with the programming and you can either browse (when you are not certain of the title of the show) through the website's programming content or use the search box the website provides (when you are confident about the exact title of the show) to jump right to the programming quickly and easily.

Browsing PBS

The PBS website takes another approach. It offers several options to locate relevant programming. It allows you to search by browsing a drop-down subject list that takes to you a listing of related programming (click here to view the Browsing PBS video; http://infogr.am/PBS-Browsing-the-Collection/). It also includes an additional "Select a Subtopic" drop-down menu list that further refines your results. A shortcoming to using this method for finding relevant programming is that it returns only results that are approximately a year old. If you are looking for older programming, this method would not work.

The other browse option PBS provides is the choice to use the "PBS Programs" link. By clicking on this link you are taken to a page showing images of the various program types that PBS offers. This can work well if you are familiar with the content produced by each of the programming channels.

Quick Tip: These methods work well only when you are looking for the most current programming materials.

For example, if you were looking for materials on tornadoes, you would need to know that *NOVA* is one of the first sites to explore. Clicking on the *NOVA* icon takes you to the *NOVA* website. Similar to the main PBS webpage, you can select a topic to browse. The weakness of this approach is that, again, it is biased toward recent and current programming. Therefore, if you are trying to locate materials on tornadoes, it would be very difficult indeed to identify the show "Hunt for the Supertwister," which aired in 2004 but has some good ILMs.

A second method is to go the educator or teacher sites that accompany many of the entertainment and educational media content. The material is generally geared toward grades K–12. Also, the organization and the method of browsing the content of these sites are not geared not toward locating ILMs but toward providing access to lesson plans or homework and related materials sorted by instructors' teaching disciplines and the grade level of the students.

Several of the aforementioned media companies and organizations have dedicated websites for educators. For example, PBS Teachers (http://www.pbs.org /teachers) is very robust, with all types of high-quality digital resources including some games and interactive resources—similar to micro tutorials. You can navigate the site through grade level and topic as well as search using a basic and advanced search tool.

The site integrates content from many PBS programs and in 2011 has begun to integrate additional learning resources through PBS LearningMedia (http: //www.pbslearningmedia.org) from other publicly funded organizations such as the National Archives, the Library of Congress, National Public Radio (NPR), NASA, the National Science Foundation, the National Institutes of Health, and the U.S. Department of Education. While ILMs currently comprise a small portion of the thousands of resources available through this site, they are of high quality.

Browsing PBS Teachers

The means by which you can search for ILMs at PBS Teachers are quite good. It has a nicely designed basic browse tool that lets you select the student grade level from the top navigation bar and then the subject or topic (click here to view the Browsing PBS Teachers; http://infogr.am/PBS-Teachers-Browsing-the-Collection/). For example, using the tornado topic, you can browse a list of related class resources by selecting the 9–12 grade level and then choose the Science & Tech topic. The results are then displayed with additional filter tools that allow you to further refine your results. There is a subtopic "Meteorology" filter and a "Media Type" filter that allows you to select "Interactive/Online Activity." By doing this, you get about a dozen results, one of which is an interactive tutorial, "Hunt for the Supertwister: Rate Tornado Damage." The tutorial teaches viewers how to rate the intensity of the tornado by the damage it causes — not surprisingly this resource was designed for the PBS *NOVA* program "Hunt for the Supertwister."

Quick Tip: *Using the browse function is not as quick as using the basic keyword search box. It is a good way to narrow down your results while not excluding possible additional relevant ILMs.*

The other method to finding ILMs at this site is to use either the basic search box or advanced search tool. Both work well. Simply typing "tornado" into the basic search box gives you over a dozen results; "Hunt for the Supertwister: Rate Tornado Damage" interactive tutorial is the second result. Selecting the advanced search screen gives the additional filters of "Media Type," "Subjects," and "Grade Level." Neither the basic nor the advanced keyword searches appear to support Boolean operators.

Another good example of websites dedicated to interactive resources for educators is Discover Education (DE; http://www.discoveryeducation.com). It is organized similar to PBS Teachers and contains many of the same types of interactive digital content. Surprisingly, DE's content is not identical to or necessarily even links to educational content developed for the Discovery Channel. For example, if you were looking for ILMs about tornadoes you would not find anything at the DE site — not even a link to the related interactives or games created for *Storm Chasers*. However, it works both ways. There is content at DE that you cannot get access to through any other site.

As discussed in the previous chapter, you can also use a college or university's search engine or a general search engine to locate ILMs. Using the site's keyword search generally works fairly well for common subjects and topics but less so with specialized ones. However, unless you are very specific and use good keywords, this method can be more challenging and time-consuming than either of the first two approaches. When using this technique you need to practice all the good searching habits and practices covered in Chapter 3.

Quick Tip: Unless the entertainment or educational website has an advanced search tool, it generally will not be as quick or as effective as using Google's advanced search tool and will limit your search to return results for only that site's content.

Basic Keyword Searching

You can perform the same search using either the keyword search box at Discovery Channel's website or Google's search engine. The results will not be identical (fewer total results using DC's keyword search), and their order will vary. The advantage to searching the site via Google instead of via the site's internal keyword search is that more search tools are available through the former, which will allow you to further refine your results.

Google's instant search is a very useful tool when searching entertainment media sites. It allows you to search a website's content very quickly and easily. You can simply type in the site you want to search, and quite often the top results will be that site with a text search box provided at the bottom of that specific result. Once you type relevant keywords into the search box and click on the search button, the results of your site search are displayed, and you can then scroll to the bottom of the results list page to access the advanced search screen provided by Google to further refine your query.

EDUCATIONAL SOFTWARE COMPANIES

The number of companies and organizations developing free or very low cost online learning resources (specifically games and activities) for elementary school-age children is exploding. Unfortunately, this has yet to translate to the widespread development of these resources for higher education students. The remainder of this chapter explores a few sites that are relevant to faculty, librarians, support staff, and students in higher education. Additionally, this portion of the chapter looks toward the future development of software companies developing learning modules/tutorials, games, and simulations for the higher education market.

A number of factors will drive the development of learning apps and edutainment online software. These trends tend to be motivated by several factors, including the need to provide additional support to students who struggle with foundational content; the need to cover more material and the rise of hybrid/blended and online courses; the need to enhance and demonstrate student learning outcomes, retention, and success; and the need to engage and increase the time students effectively spend learning. For example, instructors need students to be able to self-remediate learning gaps in college-level courses with prerequisite subjects in which they may not have adequate knowledge.

Mobile device apps are one of the most influential consumer trends that continue to push ILM growth by for-profit companies in higher education. Apple, one of the largest technology companies in the world, is leading the way in providing access to educational app development. Google and Microsoft are likely to follow Apple's lead. Again, the focus for many of the learning apps is currently geared toward K–12 children. However, students can use some educational apps for remedial instruction when they take introductory courses in college.

The App Store is the place to discover Apple's paid and free educational apps. Some of these do not fit the definition this book uses to define ILMs, but you can find some tutorials, learning games, and basic simulations.

The key to searching the App Store is to determine what approach you want to take. For example, to very quickly see what is available, what is new, and what is popular all you have to do is use the quick links and choose "Education." This will show what is popular in the category (both free and paid apps). This can be time-consuming since you have to browse under predefined categories that may or may not contain relevant materials.

Basic Keyword Searching

Another approach is to use the keyword quick search box located in the top right corner. This allows you to look for a specific type of app and will search the iTunes store and therefore will require you to refine your results. As you type in appropriate keywords, a drop-box of pertinent titles appears with related apps (not unlike Google's search terms that pop up once you type in keywords in Google's search). You can use the "Power Search" tool to further refine your results (click here to view Searching iTunes video; http://infogr.am/iTUNES-Searching/).

In the future, companies that desire to engage their customers in educational issues related to their business will develop more games and simulations that faculty and students can use at higher education institutions. A good example of this is the energy industry, which is under increasing societal pressure to become greener and to help solve the world climate change problem.

As a response to this and other pressures, Chevron partnered with the Economist Group to develop a game called Energyville (http://www.energyville .com/). It was created as a tool to educate people about available energy sources and related economic, environmental, and security issues. This is a hybrid game/ simulation that allows you to play solo or in a group. Your goal is to completely power up your city in such a way that you lower the impact your energy sources have on the city's economy, environment, and security.

There are only three levels in this ILM; the higher your energy management score, the lower your energy impact. This type of ILM could be useful as a discussion point in classes about economics, business, and public policy. Finding this type of ILM is more challenging and generally can be done only using a search engine and practicing the search techniques covered in Chapter 3.

As illustrated in the book's preface, it is always difficult to predict the future, and the case for the development of interactive learning materials for higher education is no different. Nevertheless, these resources have already exploded on the scene for elementary educators and are increasingly created and shared with ease, so it is necessary to find successful solutions in meeting the learning challenges discussed in the first several chapters. All this means that in the next decade companies are very likely to make ILMs increasingly available to higher education. The primary form these ILMs take may be learning apps that can be downloaded to a mobile device or Web-based programs that simply load and run in a Web browser.

The Exhibitors

Museums, Professional Organizations, and Governmental Organizations

Good things only happen when planned; bad things happen
on their own.

— Philip Crosby

The educational community extends beyond traditional colleges and universities to encompass not-for-profit organizations like museums, professional organizations, and governmental agencies. These groups have been increasingly integrating interactive learning materials into their online resource offerings as educational materials for primary, secondary, and postsecondary students and educators. The overall quality of these materials tends to be quite good.

This chapter focuses on how you can identify and locate interactive learning materials (ILMs) using these sites. The first part of the chapter examines museums. The next section looks at how professional organizations are either creating or sharing ILMs for their membership. The chapter concludes with discussion of how governmental organizations like NASA and the National Science Foundation (NSF) are integrating and sharing these digital resources for educators.

The structure of this chapter is similar to the previous chapter. Keep in mind several tips as you read. First, museum sites are often organized by their exhibits. Being aware of the types of exhibits a museum offers can make locating related digital resources much easier. Also, many museums offer resources for educators to augment the exhibits they are running; these sites are excellent starting places to search for useful ILMs.

In addition, professional organizations vary widely in their use of ILMs to inform and educate their members and the public. Often these sites have sections for learning more about related topics and refer to relevant ILMs they or others have created. Governmental organizations also increasingly provide resources for and have websites geared specifically toward educators. These are often excellent starting points to find relevant ILMs.

Table 7.1
Video List for Searching Museums, Professional Organizations, and Governmental Organizations

	Video URL
Smithsonian Institute: Searching the Collection	http://infogr.am/Smithsonian-Institute-Searching-the-Collection/
PRIMO: Searching the Collection	http://infogr.am/PRIMO-Searching-the-Collection/
NSDL: Browsing	http://infogr.am/NSDL-Browsing-the-Collection/
NSDL: Basic Searching	http://infogr.am/NSDL-Basic-Search-Searching-the-Collection/
NSDL: Advanced Searching	http://infogr.am/NSDL-Advanced-Search-Searching-the-Collection/
NASA: Searching the Collection	http://infogr.am/NASA-Searching-the-Collection/

SMITHSONIAN MUSEUMS

Museums have been increasingly developing ILMs to enhance their collections and exhibits, and the Smithsonian Institution (SI) is one of the best examples. The nineteen museums and galleries, along with the National Zoological Park and nine other research facilities, comprise SI, which is the world's largest museum and research complex. Together these museums have digitized more than 6 million objects and emphasize that education is at the core of their mission. Accordingly, it should not be surprising that some of these digital objects are ILMs.

The sheer size and scope of SI is staggering and can be intimidating to anyone trying to locate a specific type of ILM for his or her course. ILMs can be located in five primary ways, and some are more effective and efficient than others: (1) using the SI main website quick search textbox; (2) the "Exhibitions" tab keyword search tool; (3) the Smithsonian Collections Search Center site; (4) the Smithsonian Educators website search tools; and (5) each individual museum's website, some of which have their own unique advanced search options page.

The quick search box (click here to view the Searching SI video; http://infogr.am /Smithsonian-Institute-Searching-the-Collection/) can be a useful tool and does have a limited ability to use some Boolean search operators. The biggest disadvantage to this search approach is that there is not an advanced search tool option. However, as previously discussed in prior reviews in this book, you can use an advanced search site like Google.

Quick Tip: The quick search box works best when you use very specific keywords to get an initial list of relevant resources. It is possible to display the order of your results by date or relevance — the search defaults to relevance.

A few basic limiters can help refine your search: related events, related books, related music, and related collections. Of these, only related collections might be useful in trying to identify appropriate ILMs. For example, if you were searching for an anatomy game you could type the phrase in quotes into the search box, and this would return a couple of results. You would not need to refine your results list with so few sites found. By using the related collections link to search the Smithsonian Collections Search Center site, you would not return any results.

The Smithsonian Collections Search Center is designed to provide easy one-stop shopping for over 7 million of the Smithsonian's museum, archives, and library and research holdings and collections. However, it is not optimized for searching ILMs. Evidence of this is seen in how it did not find either of the results returned for the "anatomy game" search while using SI's basic keyword search tool. Additionally, there is no way to limit your search to games, simulations, or tutorials/modules. In the future this tool could be quite useful for searching ILMs since it offers a number of ways to filter search results.

Another approach to locating educational ILMs is to use the exhibitions keyword search tool by clicking on the "Exhibitions" tab at the top of the site's navigation bar. However, this method is not a quick and efficient way to locate good ILMs for several reasons. For example, if you try to search for an anatomy game by typing the words "anatomy" and "game" into the keyword search box, you will get no results. This search also has its own unique delimiters, including upcoming, past, or virtual exhibitions. The search defaults to current exhibitions.

Quick Tip: You can limit a search by category types such as "Art and Design," "History and Culture," "Science and Technology," and "Kids Favorites."

If you broaden your search by simply using the keyword "anatomy," you still do not return any results under the default search of current exhibitions. However, if you click on past or virtual exhibitions you do get "Artificial Anatomy: Papier-Mache Anatomical Models," which ran in the American History Museum from May 13, 2000, to July 8, 2001. If you click on the "Online Exhibition" link, you are finally taken to the main site for this exhibit, which allows you to get to the same anatomy game returned as the top result by using the SI's quick search box from the main website.

Another way to access ILMs is to go through the "Educators" link, which provides access to the Smithsonian Education site designed to be the gateway to the museum's educational resources. Once again the bias for these resources is toward K–12. Furthermore, this site alone will not be sufficient to locate all the possible

ILMs that the Smithsonian Institute offers because it searches only about two thousand resources.

Quick Tip: This search method lets you narrow your results by grade level, subject area, and museum. Also, it lists the Boolean search operators that you can use.

If you are looking for an anatomy game through this site, you will be disappointed to find there are no results with the keyword search tool using the keywords "anatomy AND game" for this site. In contrast, conducting the search using just the word "anatomy" in the keyword search box returns almost two dozen results (whereas conducting the exact same search using the aforementioned SI quick keyword search returns more than five thousand results); this is small enough to make it possible to browse through the entire list quickly. By doing so, you would find a link to "Artificial Anatomy: Papier Mâché Anatomical Models."

You can also search each individual museum's website—some of which have advanced search options. This can be a very effective means to find ILMs, but it can be problematic if you are not certain which museum might be responsible for the topic or content that you are looking for. Additionally, many of the various museums have different search interfaces as well as different search tools.

Searching for an anatomy game illustrates the differences in using the various methods to search the Smithsonian Institute. For example, searching for human anatomy ILMs can be conducted at both the Museum of American History and the Museum of Natural History since these are two of the most likely candidates for having these interactive open educational resources. Both the Museum of American History (http://americanhistory.si.edu/index.cfm) and the Museum of Natural History (http://www.mnh.si.edu/) are similar to their parent SI website in terms of how you look for digital resources. They both have browsable and searchable collections and exhibitions and a section for educators.

What sets these two apart from their parent site is that they both use an advanced search page to refine results. Unfortunately, you cannot immediately jump to the advanced search page at the Museum of American History website. Rather, you must first use the basic keyword search tool located at the top of the museum's main page. Then after returning your results list you have the option to click on a link to conduct an advanced search, which looks very much like Google's advanced search page. Conducting a search using the basic keyword search tool with the words "anatomy AND game" returns over three hundred results, but the first result is the game design for the "Artificial Anatomy: Papier-Mache Anatomical Models" exhibit. The rest of the results are not relevant.

The Museum of Natural History, in contrast, allows you to jump right to an advanced search page. Conducting the same search using the advanced search tool with the words "anatomy AND game" returns only about thirty results, and the vast majority of links do not have anything to do with human anatomy. If you further refine your search using the keywords "human anatomy AND game" you get a few more than twenty results and one additional recommended link, which takes you right to the "Human Origins Program: In Search of What Makes Us Human." You cannot get to the anatomy game designed for the "Artificial Anatomy: Papier-Mache Anatomical Models" exhibit from this website.

Museums are not in the business of developing ILMs. However, educational learning materials they offer provide an engaging digital resource to educate people about the topics and issues related to their exhibits and collections. For this reason it is likely that museums will continue to develop and integrate ILMs into their digital resources.

Currently, the cost to use these resources is free; in the future this may change. For the time being, museums offer high-quality ILMs for educators at every level to use. One of the challenges in using these sites to find ILMs is that you have to be familiar with the collections of the museum to identify the best places to search for a specific ILM. Additionally, as discussed in Chapter 5, the search interfaces of online educational repositories and digital libraries and their effectiveness vary widely from one site to another. To locate specific museums in the United States, the American Association of Museums offers a museum search tool (http://iweb.aam-us.org/Membership/MemberDirectorySearch.aspx) to identify museums by type and then click on the returned results and go to the museums' websites. There are thousands of museums outside the United States, and these too might have valuable ILMs that can be used in higher education. For example, if you are interested in finding Canadian museums, you can use Virtualmuseums.ca (http://www.museevirtuel-virtualmuseum.ca/Search.do?mu=on) to locate over three thousand.

PROFESSIONAL ORGANIZATIONS

Professional organizations and associations exist to advance a specific profession and the interests of persons involved with or issues related to that profession. As such, these groups offer another option to locating high-quality ILMs. By searching the website of a relevant professional organization, you may find very useful ILMs. Health organizations are often good examples of professional organizations that create excellent public educational resources.

Generally, these groups are not in the business of creating ILMs, but increasingly they do some for member, public, or student education. Some organizations, such as EDUCAUSE, provide funding to develop ILMs. Additionally, some organizations seek to collect (or link to) high-quality ILMs that their membership can use for educational purposes.

PRIMO

The Peer-Reviewed Instructional Materials Online (PRIMO) database (http://www.ala.org/apps/primo/public/search.cfm) is affiliated with the Association of College and Research Libraries (ACRL), a division of the American Library Association (ALA). The PRIMO committee is part of the ACRL's Instruction Section, whose mission is to promote and share "peer-reviewed instructional materials created by librarians to teach people about discovering, accessing and evaluating information in networked environments" (ACRL Instruction Section, 2012). To this end, PRIMO created a database with instructional resources that are reviewed and selected by the committee.

The Collection PRIMO contains all types of instructional materials, some of which are ILMs. The database is not comprehensive; rather, it is meant to be small (containing only several hundred resources) and selective. This approach means that the materials selected for inclusion are very exclusive. However, its size, coupled with the fact that ILMs are only a subset of all the instructional materials it includes, means that you may not find many library-related ILMs.

Searchability PRIMO's general searchability is good. It has a very utilitarian interface that is easy to use, browse, and search (click here to view the Searching PRIMO video; http://infogr.am/PRIMO-Searching-the-Collection/). You can access the browse function by clicking on the "Browse the Entire Database" link located in the upper left on the website's home page. You can also perform a basic keyword search by using the "Search for Specific Records" link located right below the browse link. The "Search by Creation Information" link is unique to this database and will be examined later in the chapter.

Browsing PRIMO is very basic and does not allow you to choose any criteria with which to view the collection. You can browse the entire collection, which because of its small size is possible but still not desirable. The time you would invest in looking through several hundred resources is not likely to be very efficient because not many of them are ILMs.

Quick Tip: *The best method for using PRIMO's browser function is to look for the most recent submissions by sorting by date.*

It is possible to sort your results by date. Furthermore, this database does provide you with the total number of items in your browsing results. You can also choose how many results you want to display — from a minimum of five to all the records.

Records Search PRIMO's records search tool is straightforward and easy to use and offers advanced search options. It is intended to use Boolean search operators such as AND, OR, or NOT. You can use keywords in conjunction with additional criteria (e.g., description, title, author, category, audience) to help you further refine your search.

Quick Tip: *The "Category" search option allows you to identify the type of material for which you are looking. This is helpful when trying to find a tutorial. However, there are no categories for either games or simulations; therefore, you need to type these words into the keyword search to find this specific type of ILM.*

Additionally, you can sort your results by the same criteria as discussed earlier in browsing the collection.

PRIMO's returned search results default to a more detailed record type and give a number of descriptors such as title, author, URL, description, category, audience, related keywords, and date. It is not possible to further refine your returned search results. You must either redo your search using additional search criteria or use the advanced creation information search tool.

Creation Information Search   The creation information search tool is unique to PRIMO and allows you to search more nontraditional criteria when looking for ILMs. You can select limiters such as numbers of library employees involved in the creation of the resource, number of hours it took to create the project, funding received, support received, and technology used.

Quick Tip: The technology used limiter can be very helpful in identifying ILMs that are either games or simulations, since multimedia interactive plug-ins such as Adobe Flash, Shockwave, and JavaScript are often used to create ILMs.

You can also sort your results by the same criteria as in the browse and search functions. The first couple of search criteria limits seem less useful for most searchers, although it might be helpful to search for materials that required more staff and time to develop since the complexity of games and simulations often demands more effort and expertise.

Generally, professional organizations' sites are not the best place to start your search for ILMs, but they can be very useful for finding superior specialized digital resources. The best approach is to start with the professional organizations with which you are most familiar and use these resources as a secondary method to augment your search for ILMs. However, there are thousands of professional organizations in North America alone. To learn more about organizations that you can use in your search for ILMs, you can use your public or academic library or a website like GuideStar (http://www2.guidestar.org/Home.aspx), which provides a searchable index of thousands of nonprofit organizations.

GOVERNMENTAL (AND AFFILIATED) ORGANIZATIONS AND AGENCIES

Governments around the world and throughout history have played roles in the education of their citizens. Today, because of the increasing need to have a highly trained and skilled workforce, governments have been more active in their citizens' higher education. In the United States, the government both at the federal and state level is becoming more involved in promoting and assessing the use and impact of the educational initiatives sponsored or supported by their federal and state agencies.

This last section examines two exemplary U.S. government (and affiliated) sites — National Science Digital Library (NSDL) and NASA — that provide excellent digital educational resources for K–20 educators in math, science, and technology. These are the focus because the U.S. government has identified these as areas in which its citizens are falling behind the rest of the world in learning. The chapter concludes with a list of the top related sites worth investigating to find ILMs.

NSDL

NSDL (http://nsdl.org/) was created via a partnership between Cornell University, Columbia University, and the University Corporation for Atmospheric Research in 2000 with funding from the NSF. NSDL makes available various types of digital resources and collections supporting science, technology, engineering, and mathematics (STEM) education. It has extensive governmental partnerships with the NSF, U.S. Department of Education, and the Institute for Museum and Library Studies as well as with various state agencies. Additionally, nearly twenty network partners provide access to their collections through the NSDL (see http://nsdl.org/partners), making it a collection of collections. While the scope of the digital library is focused strictly on STEM educational resources, the size and quality of the collection are very impressive; it provides approximately 30,000 resources for higher education alone.

NSDL offers its resources for free and is designed primarily for faculty and students in primary, secondary, and postsecondary education. Its searchable library links to all types of online learning materials, including ILMs, and provides basic descriptions along with more detailed records. There you can access more than fifty types of online educational materials such as media, book, data sets, lesson plans, and ILMs.

The Collection (Quality, Usability, Currency, and Reliability) NSDL is one of the largest STEM digital libraries on the Web, and more than 150 unique collections share their resources there. Thus, many of its resources can be found in other online repositories or library collections, such as PhET. By becoming a central source for STEM digital resources, NSDL offers one of the best starting points for faculty to perform a metasearch for STEM-related ILMs.

Many of NSDL's 50,000 materials are not ILMs, but it contains an impressive array of over 1,400 tutorials, 600 games, and 13,000 simulations for students and faculty to explore and use. Because the resources come from educators and professional experts in the field, they are usually very high quality.

Like other repositories and libraries examined in this book, the ease with which instructors can integrate the materials into their courses depends on the technology that they have available to them. Learning management systems like Blackboard make this much easier.

The currency of NSDL's STEM materials is quite important. This makes it surprising that there are no dates or currency fields displayed with either the short or complete records of the materials. Also, there is no date added field in the NSDL. Given the time sensitivity of information related to the fields of science and technology, this seems to be a significant omission. The links' reliability does not appear to be an issue even though NSDL does not house its material.

Quick Fact: The only way to identify the date NSDL material was copyrighted or developed is to go directly to the material (and that does not guarantee that it will be provided), which can extend the time you need to search for materials in the library.

Searchability NSDL's overall searchability is fairly good. It provides two primary means by which users can search its collections: a multifaceted browsing tool; and a keyword search box with advanced search options. The following sections cover how to effectively use each of these search functions.

Browsing The browsing function of the NSDL digital library is unique and slightly more complex than most but, once mastered, is easy enough to use (click here to view the Browsing NSDL video; http://infogr.am/NSDL-Browsing-the-Collection/). The NSDL allows you to browse its collection in eight different ways, although most of these methods are not generally going to work well for identifying relevant ILMs. Browsing by "NSDL Science Literacy Maps" is a novel approach to go about guiding instructors to relevant resources, but it is meant for K–12 educators. The two most effective and efficient approaches to browsing the NSDL collections is via the "Collections" and "Resources" pages.

To browse by collections, simply click on "Collections" located on the left navigation bar under "Browse." This takes you to a page where you can choose various paths to browse the NSDL. You can use the left navigation bar to browse the collection organized by broad subject headings (e.g., biological and health sciences, geosciences, mathematics). You can also browse through an alphabetical listing of all the current partners that make their collections available in the digital library.

What sets this feature apart is the ability to browse a specific collection under an identified subject heading and then refine your returned browsable list by doing a keyword search within the parameters of the results list. For example, if you are looking for a simulation of how friction heats materials, then you could start by selecting the "For Education" tab under the "Physical Sciences" category. This would return a list of approximately a hundred partner sites, one of which is the "PhET Interactive Simulations" examined in Chapter 5. By clicking on this link, you would be presented with over a hundred results. You could then type "friction" into the keyword search box located in the top left corner of the screen. This would have returned only about a dozen results, one of which is "Friction," a simulation that demonstrates how friction causes a material to heat up and melt.

To browse the NSDL resources, use the left navigation bar under "Browse" and click on "Resources." This takes you to a page where you can choose to browse by education level, audience, resource type, and subject. Once you select a specific parameter, such as education level, you will be presented with a list of all the educational levels for which there are available resources. If you select undergraduate (upper division) you will get a results list of over 18,000 resources, which you can then further refine by using the keyword search box located in the top left corner of the screen.

Because of the size of the NSDL collection, this method is not the recommended approach for identifying ILMs. This is illustrated by using the friction example, in which choosing this approach and refining your browsable list with the keywords "friction" and "simulation" would have returned over six hundred results. The returned list of results is simply too large to browse beyond the first few pages.

One of the most intriguing methods for searching for the different types of ILMs is to use the "Resource Type" option for browsing the NSDL collections. It is important to note that this option has some limitations. For example, using the friction simulation illustration used previously, you could browse the over 13,000 interactive simulations and then refine your browsable list using the keyword search feature with "friction." However, you would still have to look through over a thousand results (although you may want the results of only the first few pages, which seems fairly precise). Another limitation of the browse method in the NSDL is that it does not allow you to further refine your results by any other means or to order your results in any form.

Keyword Searching NSDL The quick search is a simple keyword search tool located at the top center of the website. Typing in keywords related to the material you are looking for returns a list in the center of the search results page. The digital library also provides a "Search Tips" page that gives detailed information about how you can effectively search the NSDL.

Quick Tip: NSDL recognizes Boolean operators such as AND, OR, and NOT, which allow you to further refine or expand your results depending on your search needs.

NSDL gives you little control over how your results are displayed except to select the number of results returned per page. On the top left side of the results page, you will see your search keywords displayed (click here to view the Searching NSDL video; http://infogr.am/NSDL-Basic-Search-Searching-the-Collection/) as well as the total number of results. The quick search works best when you have a clear understanding of the topic of the resource you want to locate and from which you know pertinent, specific keywords. Additionally, it is possible to combine the keyword search with advanced options to narrow down your results.

Advanced Search Options The NSDL advanced search has been integrated into the "Search" box. By performing a quick search you can access the delimiters. This is the best method for increasing the precision of your search in the digital library.

With the advanced options delimiters, you can select different criteria to limit your search by grade level, type of resource, subject matter, and related pathway (click here to view the Advanced Searching NSDL video; http://infogr.am/NSDL-Advanced-Search-Searching-the-Collection/). However, it does not allow you to choose where the keywords appear, whether in the title of the material or even the description, but instead looks for keywords in multiple fields including the title and description.

Quick Tip: *Searching only the title or description fields will limit the number of results returned from your search but may not necessarily increase the precision of your search.*

For example, consider searching for a game that allows college students to interact with and learn about friction. Performing a search using the keywords "friction + game" is necessary even when using the option "Resource Type." This is because you cannot specifically select a game (or a simulation or a module/tutorial) as a resource type. Rather, they are lumped under "Instructional Materials." Additionally, to restrict results to those appropriate only for college students, select "Higher Education" for the grade level. This returns about two dozen results, which can be reviewed fairly quickly — one of which is "Funderstanding Roller Coaster" (http://www.funderstanding.com/coaster).

The Final Verdict The National Science Digital Library is a large collection of collections in the fields of science, technology, engineering, and mathematics.

Accordingly, it has thousands of quality higher education ILMs. The browse and keyword search tools work well and make it an effective and efficient source. As such, it is a very good starting point for any instructor interested in finding first-class digital resources in the STEM fields.

NASA Website

Governmental organizations over the past decade have been developing educational resources primarily for elementary and high school students, but this is beginning to change. Increasing, the high failure rate of students in higher education has been in mainstream news, and governmental organizations are beginning to explore ways they can promote their subject matter areas and educate lower and upper division students in higher education.

University faculty can use a number of governmental organizations to explore and discover high-quality online interactive educational resources, including the National Endowment for the Humanities (http://edsitement.neh.gov/), National Endowment for the Arts (http://www.nea.gov/index.html), federal and state Departments of Education, National Science Foundation (http://www.nsf.gov/), National Oceanic and Atmospheric Administration (http://www.noaa.gov/index .html), and NASA (http://www.nasa.gov). This last segment of the chapter examines the NASA website and how an instructor can locate ILMs there.

NASA has a tradition of creating and providing excellent resources for primary and secondary educators. This is reflected in thousands of teaching materials made available for elementary education students through the "Find Teaching Materials" search tool. However, a number of methods can be used to find ILMs for higher education on the NASA website. These include a quick keyword search tool, advanced search tools, a topical browsable list, a site for multimedia including interactive materials, a site for higher education educators, and the "Find Teaching Materials" search tool included in the site for educators.

With so many various means by which you can search for ILMs on the NASA website (not including also being able to use the NSDL to search for a large number of them), it is difficult for a faculty member with little experience looking for ILMs on the site to be efficient and effective in locating the resources. The two best approaches are to use the "Find Teaching Materials" and the "Advanced Search" tool webpage.

NASA's advanced search tool works well and is simple to use (click here to view the Advanced Searching NASA video; http://infogr.am/NASA-Searching-the-Collection/). It offers only a couple of options to help you refine your search. You must first conduct a quick search to access the advanced search tool. It is possible to use such limiters as all the words, exact phrase, and at least one of the words and to exclude a specific word or term. Additionally, you choose where it looks for your keywords (i.e., in the title or body of the record).

Interestingly, when you conduct a search using this method it does not give you a total count of the results returned. Rather, it displays the results in a maximum of only twenty per page. In contrast, the "Find Teaching Materials" search tool does provide a count of the relevant resources before you are taken to the results list. This can be very helpful in giving you an idea about whether you should expand your search criteria or limit it.

To access the search tool you have to click on the "For Educators" link in the top left portion of NASA's main website. Then you can select the "Find Teaching Materials" link located in the left navigation bar of the educator's site. This search tool allows you to use keywords in conjunction with limiters such as audience level, material type, and subject titles. The subject titles can be very helpful for guiding you through related topics for which NASA provides material. Unfortunately, tutorials, games, and simulations are not options under the material types listed, so you will need to type those words into your expanded keyword search box. Surprisingly, doing a similar search through both methods returns different results for each.

To illustrate this, if you want to find a simulation tool for a space shuttle launch and use the words "launch" and "simulation" you get nearly forty results using the advanced search tool and only one result using the teaching materials search tool. If you are not finding what you are seeking with the teaching materials search tool, make sure to use the advanced search tool. Conversely, if you are getting too many results with the advanced search tool, use the teaching materials search tool.

Sites like NASA should probably not be your starting point for conducting a search for relevant ILMs. This is especially true because they often have some or all of their content searchable through other venues; for instance, NASA has some resources in the NSDL. However, these sites can be good secondary sources to search in your quest for a topic specific ILM that you cannot find in a repository or by any other means.

PART THREE

Choosing and Using ILMs

To this point the book has focused on what interactive learning materials are and some of the benefits they offer as well as the most efficient process and effective means by which you can locate the best-quality learning modules (i.e., with tutorials and activities), games, and simulations. For many decades, instructors have been selecting learning resources such as journal articles and textbooks for their students. As such, a mature market ecology exists that allows faculty to search academic library databases to identify and acquire course-relevant articles and manuscripts relatively quickly and easily. A new market ecology is beginning to arise for ILMs, but it will likely be some time (at least a few years) before it becomes mature enough to make finding high-quality ILMs as easy as searching for an article on the same topic.

Choosing the most appropriate interactive learning materials and effectively using those resources to enhance student learning are vital to enhancing the student learning process. The next three chapters will examine some basic and best practices for effectively choosing the right type of ILM for your students, enhancing student interaction and time on task, and properly evaluating the impact these resources are having on student learning in your course.

The Selection Process

How to Choose and Evaluate ILMs

If the process is right, the results will take care of themselves.

—Takashi Osada

The process of finding a good peer-reviewed article on almost any topic today is relatively simple and straightforward. Knowing the right periodical database or journal to search quickly leads to you finding several if not hundreds of possibly high-quality articles through an academic library. If you are unaware of what source to search to find a particular article, a librarian is available to guide you to the best online databases at your college or university. As this book describes in detail, there is no simple process, service, or source to quickly and efficiently lead you to all the good interactive learning materials (ILMs). Likewise, choosing an ILM for your students is not as simple as reading and selecting a good article for them.

Once you know how to locate the various types of ILMs, you still need to determine which would be most beneficial to assist or enhance your students' learning of the topics and content of your course. Consider several steps before searching

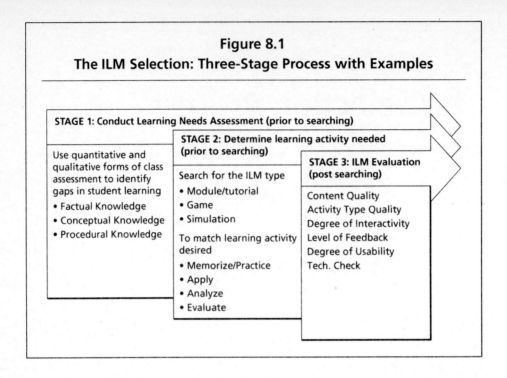

Figure 8.1

The ILM Selection: Three-Stage Process with Examples

STAGE 1: Conduct Learning Needs Assessment (prior to searching)

STAGE 2: Determine learning activity needed (prior to searching)

STAGE 3: ILM Evaluation (post searching)

Use quantitative and qualitative forms of class assessment to identify gaps in student learning

- Factual Knowledge
- Conceptual Knowledge
- Procedural Knowledge

Search for the ILM type
- Module/tutorial
- Game
- Simulation

To match learning activity desired
- Memorize/Practice
- Apply
- Analyze
- Evaluate

Content Quality
Activity Type Quality
Degree of Interactivity
Level of Feedback
Degree of Usability
Tech. Check

for and selecting the best or most appropriate ILMs for your students. The general three-stage process (Figure 8.1) for selecting good interactive learning materials involves (1) identifying your students' most significant learning needs or gaps as they relate to your course learning objectives; (2) determining the most suitable learning activity (e.g., module with practice exercises, game, or simulation) and the corresponding ILM most appropriate to meet that need; and (3) evaluating the resources you have discovered using the five key components of an ILM explained in Chapter 2 and performing a technology check, or usability testing on the identified ILMs, which ensures that they work as advertised. Stages 1 and 2 are done prior to searching for ILMs, and stage 3 is done after discovering ILMs.

Following these initial steps will help you select the best ILMs to facilitate the learning outcomes that you have for your students.

INTERACTIVE LEARNING MATERIALS NEEDS ASSESSMENT—STAGE 1

First (and most vitally) determine where your students need the most help in learning the essential and significant information and concepts in your course.

This sounds like a simple process: after all, once you have taught a course several times you quickly begin to get an impression of which concepts and topics tend to be the hardest and most difficult for many of your students. However, to do this well you need to conduct a basic class and student needs assessment. You can employ a number of qualitative or quantitative methods to gain a deeper and clearer understanding of your students' unique learning needs (Angelo and Cross, 1993).

The most comprehensive approach is to conduct a complete course needs assessment for your students, which requires you to redesign or improve upon an existing design of an entire course (Powers and Guan, 2000). Obviously, this is a quite involved process and is intended to help you make informed decisions, set appropriate priorities, and effectively and efficiently allocate resources for an entire course design. Not surprisingly, this is a very in-depth and time-consuming process that goes well beyond integrating a few specific ILMs into your course. The case study at the end of the chapter is a real-world example of how ILMs can be integrated into a course as part of designing the entire course.

Most instructors will not have the time or staffing resources to conduct a complete class and student needs assessment for their entire course. Accordingly, this chapter focuses on how to do a basic ILM needs assessment. This finite process allows instructors to quickly integrate a few strategically identified ILMs into their course to enhance students' ability to learn difficult topics and complex ideas. To accomplish this it is imperative to understand what the students' deficiencies may be and what may be inhibiting their comprehension of the material. Thus, instructors must recognize that a problem (or need) exists before it can be solved. A need is present when "there is a discrepancy or gap between the way things 'ought to be' and the way they 'are'" (Burton and Merrill, 1991, p. 21).

Applying this explanation to the selection of digital learning materials will help you decide and prioritize what content is most suitable for using ILMs to enhance student learning. Additionally, this process can assist you in deciding what type of learning activity might be most beneficial as well as what stage of the learning process (e.g., remembering, applying, or creating) is desired. A very simplistic example of this process is the concept of addition in math. If students are unable to solve the equation $1 + X = 2$, then they cannot successfully achieve a basic math course's learning objective for addition. This is a clearly identifiable gap in students' understanding and what is expected of them.

Since such a gap in understanding of a critical, fundamental concept would prevent students from being successful in current or future math courses, as the instructor you would rate the mastery of such knowledge as a high priority. As such, this content would be a good candidate for finding an ILM to enhance the students' learning. What type of ILM should you look for: game, simulation, or tutorial? To answer this you need some idea as to why some of the students in your course are struggling to learn this concept.

This is where the needs assessment can help you identify some of the probable causes for the gap in student learning, such as not enough time on task (practice) or misunderstood or missing prerequisite knowledge (Moseley and Heaney, 1994). Based on the results of your needs assessment you could then better decide what activities would best facilitate student learning. If lack of practice is a significant factor in lack of student performance, then a game-based ILM that encourages and engages the students while increasing their time on task could be a good solution.

In the previous math example, an examination of student performance on a test or quiz about addition would quickly show the level of student understanding. However, many of the gaps in student learning that you encounter in your course are more complex and will not always be easily identifiable in this manner. Therefore, there are additional ways to conduct an ILM needs assessment (Table 8.1).

Table 8.1
Needs Assessment Checklist

Needs Assessment Instruments	Type	Nature
Previous Exam Results	Quantitative	Summative
Current Test or Quiz Results	Quantitative	Both
Student GPA	Quantitative	Summative
Student Skills Surveys	Quantitative	Formative
Student Precourse Perspective Surveys	Qualitative	Formative
Student Postcourse Perspective Surveys	Qualitative	Summative
Homework Activities	Both	Formative
In-Class Activities	Both	Formative
Student Interviews	Qualitative	Both
Student Focus Groups	Qualitative	Both

The ILM needs assessment instruments fit broadly into the following four categories: (1) prior or posttest and quiz results; (2) homework and classroom activities performance; (3) course and assignment survey feedback; and (4) course interviews and student focus group feedback. It is not necessary (or practical) to conduct a complete ILM needs assessment using all of the instruments from each of the four categories. It is recommended that you conduct an ILM needs assessment using instruments from at least two of the categories and preferably mixing in one quantitative and qualitative instrument. Ideally, you will have already been using some of the needs assessment instruments (Table 8.1) in your class and can simply use them to identify the most significant, regularly occurring gaps in student learning and understanding in your course. Hopefully, the instruments will complement each other and the identified gaps in student learning will be consistent. If you ascertain conflicting results among the ILM's needs assessment instruments, then you will need to conduct additional assessments using instruments that should corroborate what the most significant student learning gaps are in your course.

DIGITAL LEARNING MATERIALS LEARNING ACTIVITIES—STAGE 2

Once you have identified and prioritized the most significant learning gaps for your students, you need to determine what type of learning activity would be best suited to facilitate and enhance student learning given the existing learning gap. Each type of ILM has its own instructional strengths, and not every one is suitable for a given identified learning activity outcome.

Tutorials that integrate practice exercises tend to focus on allowing students to understand and apply the concepts or knowledge they are learning. These can be useful in the inverted or flipped classroom approach (EDUCAUSE, 2012). Games can be very effective in reinforcing learning and helping students remember content; higher-order cognitive games allow students to apply, analyze, and at times create. Simulations are well suited for allowing students to apply, analyze, and evaluate the concepts and processes you want them to learn.

ILMS AND BLOOM'S (REVISED) TAXONOMY

Bloom's taxonomy was developed in 1956 and has been used in higher education for decades to define and scaffold course learning goals and objectives that students are to learn through course instruction. It was revised and updated by Lorin Anderson and David Krathwohl in 2001 (Krathwohl, 2002; Anderson, 2009).

Interactive learning materials should never be used in a vacuum. It is important to locate and choose the ones that are most congruent with a course's learning goals and objectives. This section examines how applying Bloom's revised taxonomy can be useful for determining the knowledge dimension as well as the cognitive process that the ILM is intended to affect. This section directly correlates to the second stage in selecting an ILM (i.e., the learning activity).

There are two dimensions to Bloom's revised taxonomy: cognitive process and knowledge. The new terms of the cognitive process dimension are defined as follows:

Remember: Retrieving, recognizing, and recalling relevant knowledge from long-term memory

Understand: Constructing meaning from various types of information through interpreting, exemplifying, classifying, summarizing, inferring, comparing, and explaining

Apply: Carrying out or using a procedure through execution or implementation

Analyze: Differentiating and organizing material into essential components, determining relationship of the parts to one another and to an overall structure or purpose

Evaluate: Making judgments based on criteria and standards through critiquing

Create: Putting elements together to form a coherent or functional whole; reorganizing elements into a new pattern or structure through generating, planning, or producing

The revised knowledge dimension is defined as follows:

Factual knowledge: Basic or foundational terminology related to the discipline

Conceptual knowledge: Classifications, principles, theories, models, and structures

Procedural knowledge: skills, techniques, and criteria for determining appropriate procedures

Metacognitive knowledge: strategic, contextual, conditional, and self-knowledge

Different types of ILMs tend to focus on different cognitive dimensions of learning. Lower-level courses that teach foundational knowledge generally emphasize more on students' ability to remember, understand, and apply factual, conceptual, or procedural knowledge (lower-order learning). Upper-level, advanced courses tend to focus more on having students analyze, evaluate, and create metacognitive knowledge (higher-order learning). ILMs can be used for both types of learning based on the instructor's desires.

Modules that include multimedia tutorials and practice exercises tend to focus more on enhancing the learners' ability to remember, understand, and apply factual, conceptual, and procedural knowledge (lower-order learning activities). Tutorials are most effective for "presenting factual information, for learning rules and principles, or for learning problem-solving strategies" (Alessi and Trollip, 1991, p. 17). Games are generally well suited for applying, analyzing, evaluating, and at times creating both conceptual and procedural knowledge (higher-order learning activities). Simulations focus most on applying, analyzing, and evaluating procedural knowledge (higher-order learning activities).

ILMs should always be integrated into courses with the intent that students will be able to do something (e.g., remember, understand) with the related course content or topics. To effectively integrate ILMs into your course it is important to have clearly defined learning objectives so that you can match the two. To map the ILM to the desired dimensions and student learning outcomes, use the chart shown in Table 8.2.

For example, if you want your students to remember the periodic table (factual knowledge), then you might want to find a game-based ILM because it could be an effective pedagogical approach to increasing student engagement with the elements. Furthermore, students may find the game an interactive fun environment that they likely will enjoy playing, thereby promoting their time on task and reinforcing their memorization of the elements, moving them from short-term to long-term memory.

INTERACTIVE LEARNING MATERIALS EVALUATION CRITERIA—STAGE 3

After determining the most significant learning gaps in a course and identifying some of the desired learning activities to help address those gaps and enhance student learning, you can use a six-step process (Figure 8.2) for evaluating the degree of appropriateness of identified ILMs to be integrated into your course.

Table 8.2

A Model of Learning Objectives (CELT Learning Technologies at Iowa State University, 2012)

Knowledge Dimension	Cognitive Dimension					
	Remember	Understand	Apply	Analyze	Evaluate	Create
Factual Knowledge						
Conceptual Knowledge						
Procedural Knowledge						
Metacognitive Knowledge						

ILM Content Quality

The first step in evaluating an identified ILM is to determine the quality of content. When considering whether it is appropriate or correct, you will want to make sure that the information the resource presents is valid. Obviously, if there is any invalid or incorrect information, the ILM should not be used.

Additionally, how the information is presented and structured and the appropriateness of the examples, models, charts, figures, and illustrations should be considered. Also think about whether the learning objectives—either explicit (this is best) or implicit—directly align with your learning objectives. If the learning objectives are a precise match, then there is no additional work on your part. However, if the learning objectives for both your course and the ILM do not match up, you will need to clarify that for your students so that they are not confused and unintentionally focus their attention on different or inappropriate learning objectives.

ILM Learning Activity Types

The second step entails examining and identifying the decision-making activities (i.e., Step 6 of Gagne's Nine Events of Instruction: elicit performance) associated with the ILM, such as drill-and-practice exercises, case studies, and games.

Figure 8.2
ILM Evaluation Six-Step Decision Tree

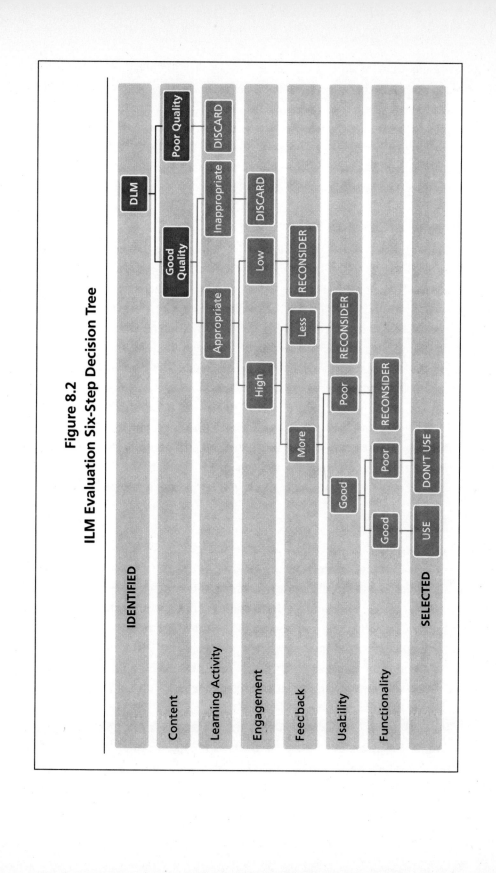

These should promote student understanding, application of concepts, analysis of concepts, evaluation of concepts, or the creation or development of new information (Krathwohl, 2002). It is important that you determine if the learning activities associated with the ILM match the type and nature of the learning process you believe will most benefit your students' progress. This phase lends itself well to partnering with an instructional designer or faculty support personnel from a center of teaching and learning excellence.

ILM Degree of Interactivity

The third step involves assessing the level of student engagement that the ILM requires or encourages. This is related to the nature and type of learning activities built into the ILM. Some learning activities require more active engagement with the content than others. Ideally, the ILM will require performing certain tasks and actions when navigating or progressing through the content. Generally, the more interaction students need to have to progress through the ILM, the better.

When students can simply click through the content (low level of engagement) and passively listen to, watch, or read, their attention may wander (especially in an online environment), which reduces their time on task. Additionally, does the ILM include rich interactive media that students will find appealing as well as address their different learning styles? Certainly, students will be more likely to want to spend more time concentrating on and engaged with the ILM if its environment is more immersive with multimedia and it is entertaining or compelling.

ILM Built-In Feedback

The fourth step examines the nature and extent of the ILM's feedback (i.e., Step 7 of Gagne's Nine Events of Instruction: informative feedback). The more detailed and customized the feedback is that students receive as they progress through an ILM, the better. It is critical to remember that feedback will allow students to know all or at least some of how they are progressing and their level of understanding and will allow for further explanation or clarification of what may still confuse them. The feedback component allows students to be more aware of how confident they are in understanding the content and provides some satisfaction as they successfully complete the ILM.

If students are not performing well, then the feedback can help guide them to additional resources or serve as motivation to talk to the professor or other students about their misunderstandings. Generally, the more learning activities engage students, the more likely it is that the ILM will have robust feedback. What form the feedback takes can be important, too. Is the feedback audio, text, or visual? How detailed is the feedback? Is it giving only basic information like success or failure (e.g., good job, sorry you got that wrong)? Can it be adaptive and guide the students based on the answers or responses they provide? All of these factors should be considered when selecting an ILM to include in your course.

ILM Usability

The fifth step in evaluating an identified ILM is to examine its ease of use to confirm that students will not have trouble navigating it. Consider whether the game or simulated process is intuitive and makes sense so that students do not have to spend a great deal of time learning how to use it. The focus should always be on the content first; the procedure by which the students use the ILM should be ubiquitous. The design, layout, and navigation of the resource should be simple, and any complexity should reside in the topic and content of the resource. Other things to consider are whether the ILM's linear or nonlinear structure confuses the learner, whether learners can become lost in its use (versus what it is trying to teach), and whether using it requires significant training and documentation.

ILM Tech Check

The final step requires checking the ILM's functionality and potential technical issues. This is increasingly less problematic because many ILMs are now designed and developed in compliance with industry standards. Furthermore, the types of software programs that are used to create Web-based ILMs tend to work well with the most common Web browsers and operating systems. One notable exception is Adobe Flash: modules, games, and simulations created with this software will not play on Apple products. This is a significant problem since so many ILMs are developed with this technology and in an increasingly mobile computing world students will be using iPhones and iPads more and more. Additionally, accessibility for hearing- and visually impaired students should be considered if applicable to anyone enrolled in your course. Many ILMs will also state the types of computer hardware and software systems for which they are optimized as well as the Web browsers with which they work best. It is important to pass this information on to your students. Other considerations when examining functionality of ILMs are how much flexibility is built into the resource, whether the ILM requires the learner to have to download any special software to use it, and whether the link to the ILM is reliable and static.

SYNOPSIS

This chapter focuses on the three-stage process of selecting the most appropriate ILM to integrate into your course resources. This involves identifying student learning needs, determining the best learning activity to promote student learning, aligning ILMs with course goals and objectives, and evaluating the quality and usability of the educational resource. Assessing the learning needs of your class and students is crucial because by using assessment instruments (e.g., exam and quiz results, surveys, student focus groups) you will be able to better determine the area within your course with which students struggle the most. Determining the activity most suitable for facilitating or enhancing your students' learning is central to the process of choosing the most appropriate ILM because each type employs unique instructional strategies and activities. Your goal should be to integrate the best available ILM into your class. Finally, it is essential to evaluate these ILMs based on their quality of content, appropriateness of learning activity, level of engagement, extent of feedback provided, ease of use, and functionality and technical requirements.

CASE STUDY

This case study gives an overview and a real-world example of an interactive learning materials needs assessment conducted as part of the comprehensive design and development of a chemistry hybrid course. The Berks College of Pennsylvania State University is a four-year commuter and residential undergraduate college with approximately 2,800 students. It is located outside of Reading, Pennsylvania.

In 2005, Berks was looking to identify a course that could be redesigned in a hybrid (i.e., blended online and face to face) format (Garrison and Norman, 2008; Picciano, 2009). The college's leadership decided that the criteria for selecting a course would include high enrollment and general education courses that had both high failure rates in conjunction with high student dropout numbers. The goal of the hybrid course redesign was to improve student performance in the selected course. Introduction to Chemistry (course 110) was identified on a short list of courses that met these criteria.

The administration then invited the chemistry department head and relevant faculty to join a team composed of the College's Center for Learning and Teaching (CLT) staff (the director, an instructional designer, and multimedia specialist) and the director of planning, research, and assessment. This very large project required that the team spend approximately a thousand hours spread over eighteen months to complete it. This case study examines one aspect of that project: the integration of both freely available, previously existing ILMs and the development of modules (consisting of tutorials and practice exercises) and a basic simulation.

The first phase of the project focused on performing a learning analysis where the instructor must clearly (and explicitly using or developing course learning goals and objectives) identify what the students are to learn in the course. This student learning analysis also examined the student population for this project. Summative survey instruments and student focus groups were employed to look at instructors' and students' perceptions with the chemistry course. This phase was more detailed and complete than is required for the ILMs' student needs assessment; however, the overall process is similar.

Next, the project team focused on identifying the learning objectives with which most students consistently struggle by scrutinizing test scores and interviewing students from previous classes (quantitative and summative). By examining and mapping the course objectives and learning outcomes to students' test scores and then comparing them, the team was able to determine how well course learning objectives were being met. Where a correlation was found between the lack of student success and a specific learning objective, the team decided that students needed additional remediation to increase their success with learning the identified course objectives. This was guided by the knowledge gleaned through the learner analysis phase, which showed that student success was impacted by their ability to recall important prerequisite course content and to come to class prepared.

The team's informed approach was to explore various ways that could facilitate student engagement with the course content both inside and outside the classroom (Gagné, 1985; Chickering and Gamson, 1987). This took the form of interactive, digital class guides, of which one significant component was ILM integration.

As mentioned already, the team believed that enhancing student interaction and engagement with course content was vital to enhancing student learning as demonstrated in increased student test scores and student course retention.

To accomplish this, a number of course enhancements were made: a student response system in class for drilling, practice, and testing; quizzes outside of class through the learning management system (ANGEL) and embedded in the class guides; peer groups with associated mentors; mini podcasts of the most challenging course concepts embedded in the class guides; preclass assignments through ANGEL and embedded in the class guides; and ILMs integrated into ANGEL and embedded in the class guides.

The hybrid course design team decided to create a new Web-based, interactive, and multimedia class guide (Amaral and Shank, 2010). Its purpose was to direct students to the most essential course content and correspondingly related learning activities. It was structured with a table of contents, topic and chapter learning goals, action items, and a learning resources page. The class guide clearly identified, scaffolded, organized, and allowed students to practice and interact with critical course content. One of its fundamental components was the integration of various ILMs, which the team selected using the following criteria and process.

Initially, the team's faculty members evaluated the content and type of textbook-provided supplemental resources, which led to the discovery that there were no ILMs. The team then investigated and sought freely available Web-based ILMs that addressed the most important learning goals identified in the analysis phase.

The chemistry faculty members reviewed the resources' content to determine their quality and appropriateness. If they passed the faculty's content quality standard, they were then examined for the type of learning activity integrated into the resource (e.g., demonstration and drill/practice exercises). If the learning activity matched what the instructors wanted their students to do, then the team discussed the ILM's level of engagement. The goal was to select the resources that provided the most effective student engagement (e.g., active learning, multimodal information input and output matched for multiple learning styles) (Ainsworth, 2006).

Then the team looked at whether the feedback built into the ILM was sufficient. If it successfully passed all these stages, then usability testing was done to make sure students would not find the resource too complex or unappealing to use and would not encounter problems navigating and using the associated components of the resource (e.g., buttons, links, menus, design layout). Finally, the selected ILMs were tested on various computing platforms (i.e., Windows Vista, XP, Mac OS) and Web browsers (i.e., Microsoft Explorer, Mozilla Firefox, Apple Safari) to make sure that no technical problems might prevent a student from using the resources outside of class or in the computing labs on campus.

GOING FURTHER: RECOMMENDED READING

Bloom's Taxonomy

Anderson, L. W. *A Taxonomy for Learning, Teaching, and Assessing: A Revision of Bloom's Taxonomy of Educational Objectives.* New York: Longman, 2009.

Marzano, R. J., and John, S. K. *The New Taxonomy of Educational Objectives.* Thousand Oaks, CA: Corwin Press, 2007.

Berks Chemistry Hybrid Course Redesign Project

Shibley, I., Amaral, K. E., Shank, J. D., and Shibley, L. R. "Designing a Blended Course: Using Addie to Guide Instructional Design." *Journal of College Science Teaching*, 2011, 40(6), 80–85.

Amaral, K. E., and Shank, J. D. "Enhancing Student Learning and Retention with Blended Learning Class Guides." *Educause Quarterly*, 2010, 33(4). http://www.educause.edu /EDUCAUSE+Quarterly/EDUCAUSEQuarterlyMagazineVolum/EnhancingStudent LearningandRet/219137.

The Implementation Process

How to Instruct and Engage Students through ILMs

> *Teaching by design includes instruction. Indeed, instruction has a central place in teaching . . . Good instruction is precisely directed at the elements of the skill involved. As a student masters the skill, he or she will find ways to go beyond the instruction or to work variations within the instruction. But here is a key point: instruction is a highly directive act. It is intentional and specific.*

— Gloria Durka

We are all familiar with the label "Warning: use only as directed," attached to most products we purchase today. Most online resources do not come with such a label. Nevertheless, it is important to pay attention to how you employ the interactive learning materials (ILMs) you desire to integrate into your course. This chapter explores how to integrate ILMs using existing technologies and examines some of the teaching pedagogy and strategies associated with ILMs.

It looks at some of the best practices of undergraduate education and discusses what you can do to maximize the impact and success of using high-quality ILMs in your course.

How you go about integrating selected ILMs into your course can play a significant role in determining whether students are successful in adopting and using them. Since ILMs are online digital educational resources, they can be made available in a multitude of ways, some of the most common of which are a course blog, Wiki, general website, social networking site (e.g., Facebook, Twitter), and learning management system (LMS).

THE LEARNING MANAGEMENT SYSTEM AND ILMS

The LMS is the most common way to make ILMs available to college students, since most colleges and universities have adopted one. An emerging trend is for LMS companies to provide free, Web-based, open-source LMSs to faculty in higher education. The downside to this approach is that faculty can become dependent on an unsupported, proprietary LMS and not be able to get local technical assistance or easily migrate their content to another platform.

Overall, these learning management systems make it easy to create an online course presence that allows you to share resources with, communicate with, and assess your students. Most LMSs allow you to do this similarly. For example, a syllabus section, a section for course lessons or modules, and a library or course reserves section are all quite common. How you organize and structure the content of your course in the LMS can impact ILM student use.

ILMs can be integrated into your LMS course in a number of ways. The following sections provide general overviews; the end of the chapter lists resources with step-by-step directions to using each of them. Remember that the manner in which you structure and label your course content, folders, or modules should be consistent with and based on how you generally organize your course, which is often reflected in the course syllabus.

The Syllabus Approach

One approach is to directly link the ILMs you want your students to use in the online course syllabus component or section. This could take the form of a Microsoft Word, Adobe PDF, or Google Docs file containing clickable links to the ILMs. This method works well if your students use your syllabus as a daily or weekly guide to check and complete course assignments. Students should not use this method alone because they may inadvertently forget to complete the ILM assignments.

The Class Guide or Agenda Approach

A less common but excellent approach is to guide your students' use and access to ILMs by integrating them into a daily or weekly class agenda or study guide (Amaral and Shank, 2010). This makes it easy and convenient for students to identify what ILMs they need to complete for class. This is a more time-intensive process than simply adding the links into your already existing syllabus, but doing so enables you to add additional directions and information that can help students identify the most important concepts and navigate the activities in your course.

The ILM Folder Link Approach

One of the simplest approaches to integrating ILMs into your course is to create one folder under the lessons tab or modules section of an LMS that contains all the ILMs your students will need to use for the course. You can do this quickly and easily by adding a link to the ILM in the appropriately identified folder, such as interactive online course homework, activities, or assignments. The downside to this approach is that you separate the resource from the rest of your course content and force students to remember to navigate to a specific section of your course just for accessing the ILMs. While you might prefer to organize your content folders by the nature of the work (e.g., readings, quizzes, assignments), students might inadvertently focus on something they perceive as more important, like tests, to the exclusion of other resources, like ILMs. Also, this is the least integrative of all the approaches.

The Lessons or Modules Link Approach

If you like to organize your course by time, such as weekly or daily, then it is critical to create folders or modules that reflect and contain all the resources, assignments, and tests for that class session and time period. If you prefer to organize your courses by subject or topic, then make sure all the related resources and assignments, including ILMs, are in the associated and appropriate folder or module. When using this approach, be careful not to confuse students about the time frame they have to complete the assignments. This method usually requires nesting folders and increases the number of clicks necessary for students to access the resource.

As already mentioned, the LMS is not the only means to provide access to your course ILMs. A good practice is to make them available through more than one means. Remember, whatever method you take to making ILMs accessible to your students, you should make sure it fits the two most important criteria: ease of access (fits the student routine) and convenience (three clicks or fewer away). Students develop course routines and habits, and it is important to ensure that your course's structure facilitates the ease with which they can access its resources. Additionally, it is critical that students are not forced to navigate your online course to access the ILMs. If they have to click numerous times to find and then access an ILM, then they will be less likely to complete the assignment.

ILMs ENABLE VARIOUS INSTRUCTIONAL APPROACHES

Technology allows you to change your instructional approach for presenting course content to your students. LMSs such as Blackboard, Canvas, Desire2Learn, and Moodle now allow faculty to share all types of digital course information very quickly and easily with students. As discussed already, ILMs, like any other digital Web-based content can be linked to and shared through these systems, which enables faculty to enhance the resources students have beyond the classroom.

ILMs Align with First Exposure and the Classroom Flip

The idea of exposing students to class lecture content prior to presenting the material in class so that instructors can use class time for more active learning approaches is not new (Walvoord and Pool, 1998). Instructors now have greater flexibility over how they deliver all the required course content. Thus, ILMs can play a significant role in moving content outside the class, which frees up time to integrate more active learning pedagogies in class. ILMs can therefore significantly impact the types of instructional strategies and teaching approaches instructors use in their courses (Figure 9.1). ILMs such as tutorials with practice exercises can be useful for those who desire to change their teaching style from lecture based (i.e., the sage on the stage) to interaction based (i.e., the guide on the side). Because students will come to class better prepared to learn, instructors can better assess during class, using a student response system or online survey

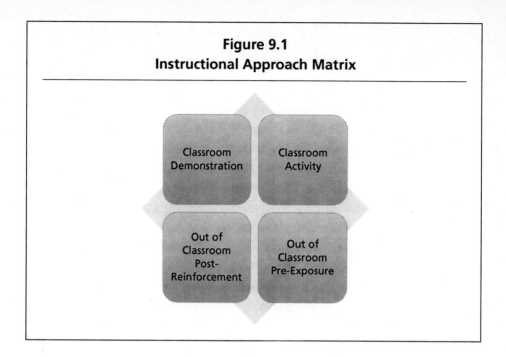

Figure 9.1
Instructional Approach Matrix

Classroom Demonstration

Classroom Activity

Out of Classroom Post-Reinforcement

Out of Classroom Pre-Exposure

tool like Polleverywhere.com or Polldaddy.com, what students understand and on which topics they may still need additional instruction.

ILMs expose students to course material and content the best because they actively engage learners. In contrast, having students simply read a chapter in a textbook, listen to a podcast, or watch a video requires them only to passively receive information. A significant challenge educators face today is that of gaining students' attention. They are surrounded by and bombarded with information constantly and are increasingly comfortable multitasking. This environment breeds student inattention. Learning resources that do not require interactivity and engagement are less likely to receive students' attention and, therefore, are less likely to accomplish course learning objectives or to facilitate student learning of the course content.

ILMs and Learning Remediation

ILMs should not be limited to merely course content introduction. ILMs help struggling students learn challenging course concepts and topics by giving them continual practice and feedback regarding their level of understanding. Furthermore, in courses (often upper-level) with prerequisites or that require students to have a solid understanding of the fundamental or foundational content prior to taking the course, ILMs can be critical for remediating knowledge gaps.

You probably have had students who are unprepared or cannot remember past critical knowledge. This often creates a conundrum; while you may not want to leave these students behind, you probably feel that it is not wise to take valuable class time to review concepts in which the majority of the class is already confident. This is an ideal situation in which ILMs can be used to remediate the learning gap. Tutorials with practice exercises allow students to review and practice content at their own pace and on their own time. These same resources can then be used to monitor and gauge student understanding. If they are still reaching to learn the content, you can always direct them to a university or college learning services center.

Most higher education classrooms are equipped with technology such as podiums that allow faculty to use an Internet-ready computer and a projector to connect to their course through a learning management system and display it for all the class to see. This gives you the ability to bring ILMs right into your classroom. This is amplified even more when a classroom is equipped with student computers, laptops, or tablets. Additionally, when ILMs are combined with interactive whiteboards or 3D Internet-enabled TVs they can become a very engaging tool for students.

You can use ILMs as interactive classroom activities, demonstrate complex processes, and encourage team-based learning. By bringing ILMs into the classroom, you can guide students in their use of the resource. This can be especially important if the ILM is not simple and easy to use. Sometimes simulations are complex enough that students will need additional instruction on how to use them.

ILMs Align with Principles for Good Practice in Education

ILMs can be important resources for enhancing instructional practices in your courses. You can better appreciate this by examining how well ILMs promote many of the Seven Principles for Good Practice in Undergraduate Education (Figure 9.2) (Chickering and Gamson, 1987). The importance of student motivation and involvement in the learning process cannot be overstated or exaggerated. A simple search using Google Scholar for an article about "student motivation" and "college or university" returns nearly 34,000 articles. Clearly, a lot of research and writing has focused on the importance as well as the techniques for improving student leaning motivation. The following section examines how ILMs support the seven principles of good practice.

Figure 9.2
Chickering and Gamson's Seven Principles for Good Practice in Undergraduate Education

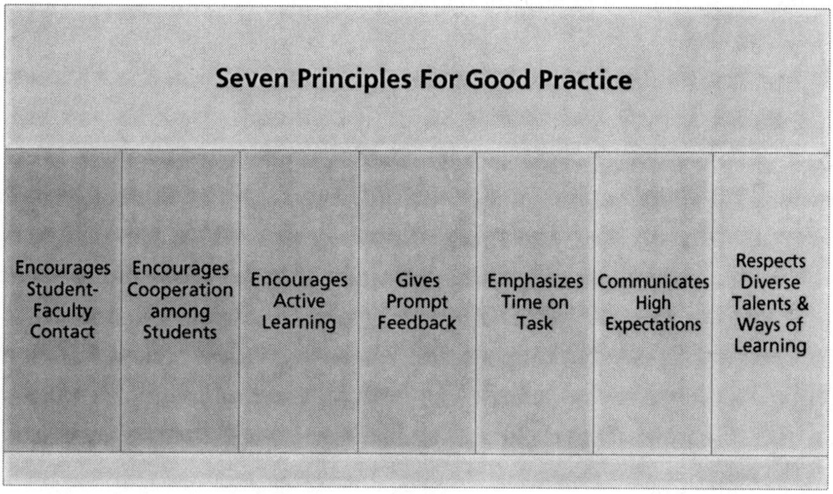

Seven Principles For Good Practice

Encourages Student-Faculty Contact	Encourages Cooperation among Students	Encourages Active Learning	Gives Prompt Feedback	Emphasizes Time on Task	Communicates High Expectations	Respects Diverse Talents & Ways of Learning

ILMs Can Encourage Student–Faculty Contact

If used properly, interactive learning materials can help faculty strengthen their contact and interaction with students. They should never be used to reduce or eliminate student–faculty contact. In an environment where hybrid or blended and online courses are proliferating, this will increasingly become a real concern, especially as administrators seek ways to reduce the cost of credit instruction. You should employ ILMs with the intent to make them critical course resources that allow your students to have more informed and intelligent conversations with you and their peers about the course and its topics. Two of the approaches and techniques you can employ to accomplish this using ILMs are (1) to take advantage of the ability that technology provides to track and get student learning analytics information about their use and success with the ILMs you use in your course; and (2) to bring the ILMs into the classroom (where you have a technology fitted and wired classroom) for use in student discussions and classroom activities.

Getting student learning analytics information from these digital learning materials can be invaluable because it tells how each student is doing and in which areas he or she is performing well and is underperforming. Unfortunately, most existing ILMs do not have this type of student learning analytics information built into them, though in the future this will likely change. Nevertheless, by embedding ILMs into learning management systems you can get some of this information, such as time on task and performance. Chapter 10 examines this in greater detail and discusses how this can be used to demonstrate improved student learning.

By bringing the ILMs directly into the classroom, you will be able to engage your students in new and exciting ways. For example, tutorials and practice exercises give you the ability to present content to the entire class that is easy to follow and incorporates more multimedia elements than a traditional PowerPoint presentation. This can save a great deal of time — you don't have to write or create any new presentation slides — when combined with an electronic whiteboard because you can stop the presentation and make comments and notes that can then be saved and posted to your course LMS site for student review. Additionally, when practice exercises are included in the ILM, you can invite your students to come up to the front of the classroom and solve them and then have a discussion about the solution with the rest of the class afterward.

If you have a computer lab classroom, by integrating games and simulations right into the classroom you can engage all of your students synchronously in the learning activity. You can then observe their performance and can lead a class discussion and evaluate the learning activity once it is completed.

ILMs Can Encourage Cooperation among Students

ILMs can also be used to enhance or promote student cooperation and interaction. Team learning can be integrated into a course in numerous ways, and the literature is replete with examples (Slavin, 1991). Games are the type of ILMs most suited to this student team and group work. By having students work in pairs or in teams to play a game, they will ideally be able to collaborate and share in the learning with their peers. This could be done either in or out of class. Tutorials and simulations often lend themselves to more individual learning, but as with games students could work in small groups to complete them.

Another instructional approach could be to assign the ILM first to students individually. After they complete it, have them next work in small groups to accomplish the same task. This is the best of both worlds: the former allows you to gauge which students are stronger and which are weaker on the topic so you can create groups to partner stronger and weaker students.

ILMs Encourage Active Learning

The term *active learning* has been extensively written about in higher education for the last several decades. There are abundant examples and techniques of *active learning* within the literature over the last several decades (Meyers and Thomas, 1993; Bean, 2011). ILMs can be very effective resources in engaging students in active learning both in and out of class. As we have examined in great detail in this book, ILMs engage students in a number of ways. Critically, a good ILM requires a student to interact with the content and activities embedded into the resource. Students should never be able to successfully complete an ILM without being required to take many actions while progressing though the resource.

This is generally not a concern with games and simulations. By their very nature, ILMs are highly interactive and require the learner to complete many tasks and actions. Learning modules (i.e., tutorials and practice exercises) are not intrinsically highly interactive, and there is no guarantee that these types of ILMs will require students to complete any action beyond navigating the content. This is why it is critical for you to evaluate the amount of interactivity these types of resources require.

For example, a tutorial that does not contain any practice exercises or activities may have a student only click through the content to progress. This type of interactivity is very limited. It means that the information is being shared in a very passive manner wherein students do not do much else besides simply watch or listen to advance through the resource. Ideally, a tutorial will include learning activities that require students to interact highly via decision-making actions and accomplishment of a task or set of tasks before progressing. Additionally, good ILMs integrate practice exercises that allow students to be engaged with demonstrating what they have learned while advancing through the resource.

ILMs Should Give Prompt Feedback

ILMs can be very useful for facilitating student feedback on important course topics and content. Chickering and Gamson (1987) appropriately assert that students need to be aware of what they know and what they do not. This helps to focus student learning and allows students to benefit from the comments and feedback about their performance. Learning modules with practice exercises are ideal for guiding, gauging, and providing feedback to students in your course.

The level of feedback can vary greatly. Ideally, you want to integrate the ILM that has more detailed and customized feedback based on the particular student response. For example, if your students need to learn how to solve complex math equations, then you would want to use an ILM that integrates practice exercises with detailed and individualized user feedback, such as an explanation as to how or why they are not correctly solving the equations. Additionally, if students repeatedly give the same wrong answer, then an ILM suggesting specific actions to take or resources to review would be helpful. Also, reinforcement can be very beneficial so that even when students solve the equation correctly they are provided feedback congratulating them and reinforcing the correct solving method.

ILMs Emphasize Time on Task

As mentioned previously in the book, numerous studies (none conducted by the U.S. Department of Education) found that student success is directly correlated to time spent doing classwork. While time on task is universally viewed as critical among faculty, it is not always easy to have students spend enough time engaged with course resources outside of the classroom. Requiring students to spend a fixed amount of time successfully completing ILMs can increase the time your students spend engaged with important course content. ILMs add in a fun factor via games and simulations, require students to pay close attention and interact with the resource to successfully complete it, require students to spend a minimum threshold of time to successfully complete them, and track student usage, interactions, and performance.

Students who really enjoy playing games or simulations will find it easier to be motivated to use the ILMs provided. Certainly, they cannot or should not always be designed solely for entertainment, but why should faculty not integrate ILMs that are good quality learning resources, especially since students find them entertaining? Most likely the commercial market will embrace this approach first, although there is some evidence that the higher education community is beginning to embrace the idea that learning games make good learning tools. For example, conducting a search using Google Scholar shows that approximately 16,000 articles have been published since 2012 on the use of games in higher education. Also, the amount of literature and studies published about games in higher education is up sharply in the last decade (Table 9.1).

Learning analytics (data and information about learners) is seen as an increasingly important tool for higher education. Institutions and instructors are being increasingly expected to demonstrate how their learning environments and instruction impacts student learning course and curricular outcomes (Johnson

Table 9.1

**2010–2001 Google Scholar Search Results
for "games learning OR higher education"**

Year	Number
2010	11,600
2009	11,000
2008	10,200
2007	8,880
2006	7,880
2005	6,600
2004	6,030
2003	4,990
2002	4,200
2001	3,410

et al., 2011). Because ILMs are digital and can reside in a learning management system, they are easily used as part of the process of gathering relevant data to demonstrate student success or lack thereof. Additionally, LMS tracking functions allow faculty to follow and get detailed information about their students' ILM use.

For example, you can examine when your students access the ILM, which illustrates whether they are waiting till the last minute before they can no longer complete the assignment or are preparing for a test. Furthermore, you can see how much time they spend using it. If it is only a few minutes, then you can infer that they got very little out of accessing the resource. The ILM may provide you with information about student performance, but if it does not have this function built into it, then you can use the LMS to create pre- and posttest assessment surveys and quizzes to determine the level of student learning. (This is examined in greater detail in Chapter 10.)

ILMs Can Communicate High Expectations

Chickering and Gamson (1987) fittingly point out that students tend to perform to the level of expectations an instructor has for them. You will generally get more if you expect more of your students. ILMs can be used to show students that you have high expectations for them. For example, games and simulations can be very challenging to successfully complete. At first, students might struggle to perform well; therefore, you can challenge them to increase their performance. Additionally, you can have students compete with themselves or other students to achieve higher scores.

Another critical component of communicating high expectations is to reward or penalize students for completing or not completing the ILM assignment. Unfortunately, we live in a world where too often students look at their grades as the sole or primary measure of their learning. When they do this, they tend to focus their attention on the assignments and tests that have the greatest weight on their overall course grades.

It is important, therefore, to assign enough weight to ILMs so that students see them as important resources for successful course completion. Also, make sure you communicate to your students how much you value the resource and explain why you feel it is important that they use it. Ultimately, to get student buy-in you must promote the ILMs as requisite and important class materials just as you would a course textbook or course pack; otherwise, it is likely that students will not see the ILM as anything more than another course resource that they do not have the time to use.

ILMs Can Respect Diverse Talents and Ways of Learning

Lastly, Chickering and Gamson (1987) point out that students have different learning styles preferences, talents, and strengths. It is important for an instructor to be able to integrate various types of instructional procedures, activities, and resources. The research on student learning styles in higher education goes back several decades (Claxton and Ralston, 1978; Kolb and Kolb, 2005) and reflects the belief that presenting materials and learning activities for multiple learning styles is best, and ILMs are often designed to do just this.

SYNOPSIS

This chapter covers the process of implementing ILMs in a course, which occurs after successfully finding and choosing the interactive, online educational resources. Several factors can influence the successful implementation of course digital learning materials, including placement, organization, and pedagogical application. The placement of ILMs into the structure of a course and the technology used to provide access to the materials are important because students have to clearly understand the role of these resources in the course as well as have an easy and convenient way to access them.

The chapter also discusses the pedagogical application of employing ILMs. Several methods were examined in detail: inverted classroom/classroom flip and first exposure; and the Seven Principles for Good Practice in Undergraduate Education. The inverted classroom discussion focuses on how you can move course content from inside to outside the classroom and the role the ILM can play in that process. The chapter concludes with a discussion of how ILMs align with and promote most of the seven principles.

GOING FURTHER: RECOMMENDED READINGS

Inverted Classroom, Classroom Flip, and First Exposure

Beagle, D. R., Bailey, D. R., and Tierney, B. *The Information Commons Handbook*. New York: Neal-Schuman Publishers, 2006.

Bowen, J. A. *Teaching Naked: How Moving Technology Out of Your College Classroom Will Improve Student Learning*. San Francisco, CA: Jossey-Bass, 2012.

Strayer, J. *Inverting the Classroom: A Study of the Learning Environment When an Intelligent Tutoring System Is Used to Help Students Learn*. Saarbrücken, Germany: VDM Verlag Dr. Müller, 2009.

Walvoord, B. E. F., and Anderson, V. J. *Effective Grading: A Tool for Learning and Assessment in College*. San Francisco, CA: Jossey-Bass, 2010.

Principles for Teaching Practice

Ambrose, S. A., Bridges, M. W., DiPietro, M., Lovett, M. C., and Norman, M. K. *How Learning Works: Seven Research-Based Principles for Smart Teaching*. San Francisco, CA: Jossey-Bass, 2010.

Davis, B. G. *Tools for Teaching*. San Francisco, CA: Jossey-Bass, 2009.

Richlin, L. *Blueprint for Learning: Constructing College Courses to Facilitate, Assess, and Document Learning*. Sterling, VA: Stylus Pub, 2006.

Weimer, M. *Learner-Centered Teaching: Five Key Changes to Practice*. San Francisco, CA: Jossey-Bass, 2013.

The Assessment Process

The Impact of ILMs on Student Learning

If you cannot measure it, you cannot improve it.

— William Thomson (Lord Kelvin)

Assessing learning can be very tricky. There is a great deal of literature about the different types of assessment, such as formative and summative (Harlen and James, 1997). Using Google Scholar and searching "higher education AND formative assessment" returns over 15,000 results; a similar search for summative assessment yields more than 10,000 results. (For several highly cited articles see Going Further: Recommend Reading at the end of this chapter.)

Since no assessment type is perfect for all learning situations and all students, a good approach is to combine several forms. Assessment is critical to the successful adoption of interactive learning materials (ILMs) in your course. If you cannot determine and measure their impact on student learning, then you have no evidence that they are effective tools for enhancing it. This final chapter examines

143

some practical approaches to integrating assessment components as well as some tips for evaluating students' perceptions of the ILMs in your course.

It is important to differentiate between assessing the student learning that takes place from using ILMs in your course and evaluating student use and attitudes toward the resources. This is not to say that there is no relationship between the two. Certainly, students who find an ILM hard to use may not be able to effectively learn with it; those who love to play a learning game might be very self-motivated and find the ILM an enjoyable and successful way to learn.

By better understanding student attitudes toward the ILMs you use in your course you may be able to more effectively integrate them and further enhance the impact they have on student learning. Likewise, discerning that students do not like a particular ILM may lead you to reconsider your choice and find something more appropriate. The case study at the end of this chapter looks in depth at some of the methods you can use to evaluate students' use and perceptions of course ILMs.

There are a number of approaches to assessing ILMs' impact on student learning, including using a pretest and posttest, employing mastery learning, using existing quizzes, mapping specific ILM content to existing midterm and final tests, and using experimental test and control groups. The following section provides a synopsis of three assessment techniques.

PRETEST AND POSTTEST

One of the best assessment methods is a pretest and posttest tool. Most ILMs do not come with a built-in pretest and posttest, but thanks to learning management systems (LMSs) this is easily rectified. Almost all LMSs have a quiz or assessment creation tool. Therefore, if you (as recommended in the previous chapter) integrate your ILMs into your class through the LMS you can develop a pretest that students can take prior to using the ILM; they can then be redirected to the posttest upon its completion.

You can employ some best practices when creating pretest and posttest instruments (Dimitrov and Rumrill, 2003). It is absolutely critical that you measure the exact learning objectives and related student learning outcomes that correlate with the ILM. Once you have these clearly identified then you want to create valid test questions. Ideally, use an already reliable and validated test instrument if you can.

If such an instrument does not already exist, then create your own. Most LMSs allow you to select multiple question formats such as multiple choice, fill in the blank, and true or false. Keep in mind that each type of test question has strengths and weaknesses.

Once you decide on the content and the type of questions, make sure that you create a large enough pool of questions so that students cannot easily cheat. Ideally, a question set will be at least twice as large as the number of questions you are requiring your students to answer. For example, if you want them to answer twenty questions, you should have the ILM draw from a test pool of at least forty. The combined length of these quizzes should not total more than a quarter of the time students will be required to complete the ILM itself. For example, if you want your students to complete an interactive tutorial that needs on average an hour to complete, then you should not create a pre- and posttest that would take longer than 15 minutes combined to complete or less than 10 minutes each.

Additionally, most LMSs allow you to randomize the selection of questions and the order in which they as well as the answers appear on the quiz (if multiple choice or select). It is critical that the pretest and posttest draw from the same pool and ask equivalent questions so that the students' learning is being measured appropriately and you are comparing apples to apples and not apples to oranges.

An advantage to using the LMS to create the pretest and posttest assessments is that you will be able to track students' use and the system will automatically grade the results for you. You do not want to provide students with any feedback after they complete the pretest prior to completing the ILM. However, you can consider this once they complete the posttest.

MASTERY LEARNING

Mastery learning is another assessment for student learning. This philosophy asserts that under the right instructional conditions most (if not all) students can learn (or master) most of what they are taught (Block, 1979). Critical to this approach is that students have the time they need to learn the content. A sufficient amount of time for each learner is critical to each learner's success. If students do not have the necessary amount of time they require to learn the topic, then they will not be able to master it. Another factor that is crucial to students' learning success is perseverance, which refers to the level or motivation and engagement they have toward the content they are learning. Students with low perseverance most likely will not master the content they are learning.

The key to using the mastery learning approach when assessing student learning with ILMs is to tie students' successful completion of the ILM to a summative test that requires them to receive a high test score (usually at least an A) before they can advance in the class. For example, students who do not score at least a 90% on the summative test would have to reuse the ILM, after which they would retake the test and continue to do so several more times until they receive an acceptable grade or need instructor intervention to help them achieve the necessary grade.

To use this method you will need to develop a summative test in the environment where you have placed the ILM, which in most cases will be the learning management system. It is critical that you require your students to take the test immediately after completing the related ILM. Additionally, you should consider all the same previously discussed recommendations for creating a posttest. Unlike the pre- and posttest approach you should consider whether you want to give the students any feedback for the answers they have given. If you decide to guide and direct them to pay special attention to certain aspects of the topic they did not understand, then make sure you have a large enough test bank so that they do not simply note the answers and plug them into the test directly the next time they retake it.

Another approach to assessing the impact of specific ILMs on student learning in your course is to have students take in-class quizzes that are timed right after they complete the ILMs and that are tied directly to its content. This way you can ensure that they are not using additional resources beyond the ILM while taking the quiz. If you already regularly use in-class quizzes to assess student learning, then this approach can be a quick and simple way to judge the impact of an ILM by comparing how well students score on the current quiz with quizzes in past course sections that did not use the ILM.

Moreover, if you have a midterm and final test in your course, you can conduct performance mapping to see what impact the ILMs may have had on the sections of the tests that cover the material for which you had students complete an ILM. To do this well you must make sure that you directly map the questions from your midterm and final test to the learning objectives of the ILM. You will need to examine comparable test scores from other course sections in previous years to see if there is an improvement in those specific sections of the tests.

THE SCIENTIFIC METHOD

The scientific method is another approach to measuring the impact of ILMs on learning in your course (Creswell, 2002; Johnson and Christensen, 2008). This method is time-consuming, complex, and fraught with challenges; therefore, it is not the most preferred method for faculty who are not planning to conduct extensive research and to publish on the topic. However, if done right the scientific method can be a very effective and compelling approach to demonstrate the impact on student learning because it can show the difference (or lack thereof) in student learning between two or more student populations.

To use this method you will need either to create a control group of students within a course or to use an entire course section of students (if you teach more than one section of a course). These students would not be allowed to use the ILMs. Some instructors may decide that they do not want to use this method because some students will not be allowed to use a resource that could help them learn.

When applied to examining student learning in an undergraduate course, the scientific method can be problematic because there can be so many uncontrolled variables within a group of students who take a course. For example, if you look at historical data from your course you may discover that students who take your course in the fall semester perform differently than students who take it in the spring because of a demographic difference in the student population. Or perhaps students who take the class during the day perform differently than those who take it at night because more nontraditional adult learners are taking the evening sections. Likewise, you may not be able to prevent your control group of students from being exposed to the ILM if they have friends in the other section who give them access to it. However, by repeating this process over time you can determine if there is a statistically significant difference between the test scores of the two student populations and demonstrate the impact that ILMs are having in your courses.

CASE STUDY: MATH 110 STUDENT USABILITY TESTING AND CALCULUS ILM EVALUATION

This case study gives an overview and a real-world example of how to assess the effectiveness of digital learning materials in an introductory calculus course at the Berks College of the Pennsylvania State University, a growing four-year commuter and residential undergraduate college of the university. The college has approximately 2,800 students and is located outside of Reading, Pennsylvania.

As part of the college's strategic plan, the college has been investigating ways to enhance and improve the teaching and learning environment for its increasingly diverse student population.

Consequently, Berks college administrators have been considering various approaches to enhancing the learning environment on campus. One particularly promising proposition put forth by the college's chief information officer was to examine and select courses that could use electronic learning (i.e., blended learning course design elements) to enhance students' learning experience.

The college administration hoped that enhancing traditional lecture courses with e-learning would boost students' learning in a measurable way and increase both student satisfaction and retention. Additionally, the administration desired to showcase several hybrid learning examples that other appropriate courses could replicate across the curriculum. Two key administrators, the chief information officer and the associate dean of academic affairs, examined all the courses taught at the college to identify introductory courses with high enrollment and particularly low success rates. Several courses were identified, and one such course was Math 110, Techniques of Calculus I.

The primary goal of this blended learning project initiative was to use appropriate e-learning elements in the college's introductory-level calculus course to enhance students' understanding of fundamental calculus topics, thereby increasing student engagement with course content; improving student test scores and course GPAs; and decreasing the overall course withdrawal rate.

Instructional Challenges

The major teaching challenges for the Techniques of Calculus I instructors are common to most college educators across higher education. Typically, a sizable cohort of students do not have a mastery of prerequisite skills and knowledge necessary to facilitate retrieval and application (e.g., power rule for exponents). Therefore, the faculty face a conundrum: how much time should they spend in class identifying and assisting students with learning this prerequisite knowledge? If they spend too much time in class reviewing this content, they may not be able to adequately cover all of their required course content.

Likewise, if the instructors do not adequately address the necessary prerequisite skills and knowledge in which students are deficient, they risk losing a good number of students who cannot successfully move forward to master the new calculus content (e.g., simplifying derivatives when the product rule is used). Additionally, faculty struggle with increasing the amount of time students spend on task outside of the classroom working on relevant course content. Consequently, students are less prepared for class, and instructors find themselves either spending far too much time reviewing the new material or simply moving on and leaving those students behind.

The Berks College administration (in alignment with the college's strategic plan) believed that blended learning might offer a possible solution to the afore-mentioned teaching challenges. The Berks College associate dean of academic affairs formed a multidisciplinary, investigatory team late in spring 2007 to begin to identify what online learning resources could be created to address these teaching challenges and meet the primary goals of the Math 110 e-learning project.

The newly formed calculus module development project team—the Berks Center for Learning and Teaching (CLT) faculty and staff, the student learning center staff, and the two primary instructors for the calculus courses—conducted a literature review of Web-based activities and modules and discussed the approaches and the implications (Hubing et al., June 2002; Kaw et al. 2003; Riffell and Sibley, 2004). This project team decided that the best blended learning approach to support and enhance student learning would be either to integrate existing interactive learning materials or to develop a series of interactive, multimedia Web-based learning modules to meet students' diverse learning needs that could be delivered via the Penn State's ANGEL course management system.

Calculus Learning Modules

Four online modules, each of which includes a tutorial and interactive practice, were completed as of spring 2009. Students view a short online tutorial, after which they are directed to an online practice exercise.

The project conducted a learning needs analysis of the Techniques of Calculus I course student population and then designed and developed the new course components. After the course was taught, the math blended learning project was evaluated using the following components: formative quantitative assessment in the form of instructors reviewing the test scores of student questions that related directly to the module content; formative qualitative assessment from students' comments and feedback from a survey that measures student perceptions of the modules; summative quantitative assessment from comparing pre- and posttest quiz scores, course GPAs, and drop rate from Math 110, Techniques of Calculus I courses prior to and after the modules' implementation; and summative qualitative assessment from end of semester student comment sheets.

While evaluation is the final phase of the blended learning project, it is repeated several times because of the iterative nature of the production process for the calculus modules. This allows students to give their perspective and input into the design of the modules, providing valuable guidance to the development team.

ILM Assessment

Assessment is the cornerstone to understanding the effectiveness of instruction, and, as is the case in this project, it guides the development of the instructional product (i.e., the calculus modules) and measures the effectiveness of these modules as a student learning aid. Furthermore, assessment enables the project team to better understand how students use and learn from the calculus modules and share these findings with other educators. To this end, the calculus module development project team integrated both formative and summative assessment into the project.

Formative Assessment

As mentioned previously, the calculus module development project team conducted formative, qualitative assessment of the modules' tutorials and practice exercises throughout the design process by surveying students in the Math 110 course at the completion of each module's component parts (i.e., tutorials and exercises). The students were asked in class to give the instructor any feedback they wish in addition to completing an online survey (Figure 10.1).

The online survey focuses on student perceptions of the instructional activities, presentation of the mathematical content, and user interface design of the modules. This student feedback informs the design and development of the modules and ensures that students' perspectives are understood and addressed (Figure 10.1). The calculus module development project team worked in close partnership with the Office of Institutional Research and Assessment at Penn State Berks to further develop and refine this survey assessment instrument.

Overall, the majority of students answered (97%) that they did like being able to practice and use the online calculus learning modules. The student survey results were consistent across all of the modules, showing that they felt that the modules were helpful and generally helped them learn the course material. They also liked the design and the ability to practice what they were learning.

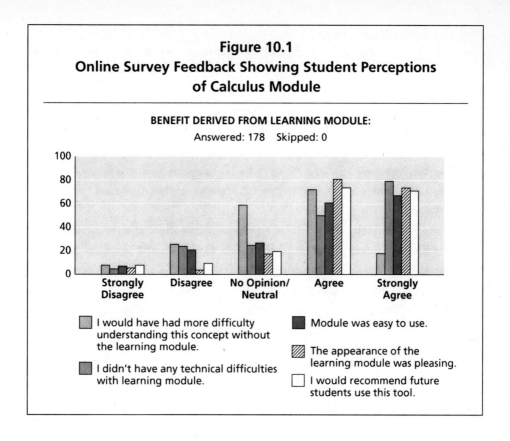

Figure 10.1
Online Survey Feedback Showing Student Perceptions of Calculus Module

BENEFIT DERIVED FROM LEARNING MODULE:
Answered: 178   Skipped: 0

Legend:
- I would have had more difficulty understanding this concept without the learning module.
- I didn't have any technical difficulties with learning module.
- Module was easy to use.
- The appearance of the learning module was pleasing.
- I would recommend future students use this tool.

Summative Assessment

The calculus module development project team decided that the best approach to measuring the impact of the course ILMs was to create pre- and posttest quizzes (Kirkpatrick, 1998). This allowed the team to measure the students' level of understanding prior to taking the calculus models with practice exercises and compare that with their level of understanding after taking the modules. To make sure the pre- and posttest quizzes were developed properly so that they could accurately measure the learning that occurred as a result of using the ILMs, the team followed the process discussed earlier in this chapter.

The pre- and posttest quizzes were created in the ANGEL learning management system employed by Penn State University. These short, multiple-choice quizzes were designed to discourage cheating by making them very low stakes and counting very little toward their final course grade. The print function was disabled so that students could not easily print out their problem set and share it with other students. Also, the quizzes were set up so that the system would randomly select a maximum of ten math problems from a pool of twenty to thirty. The quiz was timed so that students could spend no more than 30 minutes working on all ten questions. Additionally, the math problems were delivered separately, although students were permitted to skip and then return to a question if they did so in the allotted time frame. The answers for the quiz were randomized so that if students tried to compare similar problems the order of their answers would be different. Students were not allowed to see which questions they answered correctly and which they answered incorrectly for the pretest so that they could not use an answer sheet from the posttest.

The team decided that the pre- and posttest quizzes should be set up identically so that quiz design would not impact student performance. The quiz questions were designed so that students taking the quizzes would all have the same level of difficulty assigned to them. While students would not have the exact same questions asked in the pre- and posttest, it was necessary to make sure all students could get problems from the same pool of math problems so that level of difficulty remained the same. Since the LMS housed the student performance data, it was simple to look at the various calculus (Math 110) sections and aggregate the students' scores on the pre- and posttest quizzes. Across all the sections students performed better after taking the calculus modules and practice exercises. For examples, students taking Module II, Simplifying Derivatives by Factoring, performed significantly better on the posttest after completing the module than they did on the pretest prior to completing the module (Figure 10.2). The results show that students averaged a C in only one course section and a D in the remaining three on the pretest, while those same students scored an A in three course sections and a B in the remaining course section on the posttest.

This case study demonstrates that overall the vast majority of students performed significantly better on the quizzes after using the math ILM created for the introductory calculus courses at Berks. The only students who were not included in the results were those who withdrew from the course and did not complete the modules. This demonstrable evidence, combined with the fact that students performed better on the sections of the math test correlated to the content of the ILMs, convinced the math faculty that the resources were beneficially impacting students' learning in their courses. They believed that this evidence along with student feedback showed that students' perception that the resources help them learn

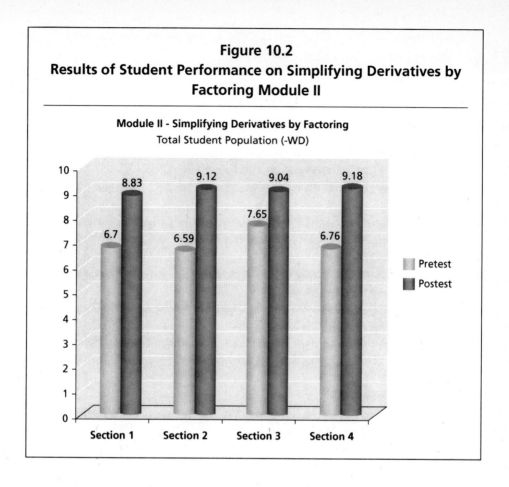

Figure 10.2
Results of Student Performance on Simplifying Derivatives by Factoring Module II

Module II - Simplifying Derivatives by Factoring
Total Student Population (-WD)

the material better aligned with the test scores showing students were performing better after using the ILMs in the course.

SYNOPSIS

This chapter covers several practical approaches—formative assessments like pre- and posttest instruments and summative assessment techniques like mastery learning—for integrating assessment components and for evaluating students' perceptions of the ILMs used in your course. Additionally, this section examines benefits and challenges of applying the scientific method to produce a quantitative and summative assessment of the impact of student learning from the use of class ILMs. The chapter concludes with a case study that illustrates some of the approaches educators can take to assess student perceptions of using ILMs and to measure their impact on student learning.

GOING FURTHER: RECOMMENDED READINGS

Formative Assessment

Banta, T. W., Jones, E. A., and Black, K. E. *Designing Effective Assessment: Principles and Profiles of Good Practice.* San Francisco, CA: Jossey-Bass, 2010.

Bonate, P. L. *Analysis of Pretest–Posttest Designs.* Boca Raton, FL: Chapman & Hall/CRC, 2000.

Nicol, D. J., and Macfarlane-Dick, D. "Formative Assessment and Self-Regulated Learning: a Model and Seven Principles of Good Feedback Practice." *Studies in Higher Education,* 2006, 31(2), 199–218.

Palloff, R. M., and Pratt, K. *Assessing the Online Learner: Resources and Strategies for Faculty.* San Francisco, CA: Jossey-Bass, 2009.

Sadler, D. R. "Formative Assessment and the Design of Instructional Systems." *Instructional Science,* 1989, 18(2), 119–144.

Yorke, M. "Formative Assessment in Higher Education: Moves Towards Theory and the Enhancement of Pedagogic Practice." *Higher Education,* 2003, 45(4), 477–450.

Summative Assessment

Biggs, J. "Assessment and Classroom Learning: A Role for Summative Assessment?" *Assessment in Education: Principles, Policy & Practice.* 1998, 5(1), 103–110.

Boud, D. "Sustainable Assessment: Rethinking Assessment for the Learning Society." *Studies in Continuing Education,* 2000, 22(2), 151–167.

Harlen, W., and James, M. "Assessment and Learning: Differences and Relationships between Formative and Summative Assessment." *Assessment in Education: Principles, Policy & Practice.* 1997, 4(3), 365–379.

Suskie, L. *Assessing Student Learning: A Common Sense Guide.* San Francisco, CA: Jossey-Bass, 2010.

How Faculty, Librarians, and Instructional Support Staff Transform Learning with ILMs in the Future

TALE OF AN ILM

Jane Doe is a faculty member in the history department at a large research university. She has been teaching for more than a decade and has witnessed many of the changes that technology has brought to her classroom over the years. She has been increasingly using her university's learning management system, Moodle, to share class resources such as her syllabus, reserve readings, assignments, and low-stakes class quizzes. Over the last several years she has noticed that more of her students have been asking her to post all of her materials (including her presentation and lecture slides) on the course website.

She had been reluctant to post all the materials there since she taught several large sections (more than a hundred students) of an introductory course in American Civil War history and wanted to encourage students to attend the lectures. Over the years she had been teaching the course, she had come to have a good understanding of the topics with which a majority of her students tended to struggle. She had tried assigning different homework assignments and additional course materials like readings and videos, but some students still struggled with remembering basic facts about the Battle of Fort Sumter.

Jane had a librarian come into her class each semester to talk to the students about the best research full-text databases that they should use when working on the final research paper for the course. At the end of one such session, Jane mentioned to the librarian, James, that she was looking for additional online library resources she could use to help students who wanted to get more information about the Battle of Fort Sumter from her course website. James asked her if she had tried integrating any open educational resources (OERs) into her course website.

Jane was familiar with the term, but neither she nor her colleagues had spent time looking to integrate these types of resources. She expressed her concern that the time it would take to find a good-quality resource had prevented her from using any OERs in her course to date. James knew some good online repositories that were well designed and easy to search and contained high-quality OERs. He offered to send her some links to the best sources with materials about the American Civil War. Jane thanked him and welcomed the opportunity to add some good resources to her course website.

Upon returning to the library, James ran into an instructional technologist, Pauline, who also worked in the learning commons of the library. Since he was aware that Pauline was interested in working with faculty to integrate interactive online resources into their courses, he mentioned his chat with Jane. Pauline immediately asked if Jane had mentioned the types of OERs she would be interested in finding. James said she had not. So Pauline asked if James could copy her in the e-mail he was going to send to Jane.

Pauline then called Jane and explained her chance encounter with James. She asked Jane what types of challenges her students were having with the course. After chatting about some of the difficulties students have with remembering facts about the Battle of Fort Sumter, Pauline suggested that an online game or simulation might make an excellent resource for helping to both motivate and reinforce the learning objectives that Jane had for the Fort Sumter lesson. Pauline explained that she could not guarantee a freely available educational game or simulation about the Battle at Fort Sumter, but she would work with James to see if they could identify any that might already exist and meet the criteria that Jane was looking for.

Afterward, Pauline went over to James's office and explained what type of resources Jane was looking for. Using the criteria that would fit with what Jane had expressed in her conversations with Pauline, James searched the various OER repositories with which he was familiar. It did not take long before James identified several possible simulations that Jane could use in her course. James sent links to these resources to Pauline and asked for her feedback and opinion about the resources he identified. Pauline reviewed and evaluated the simulations that James sent and ranked them according to the criteria: level of engagement; extent of feedback provided; ease of use; and functionality and technical requirements of the resource. Pauline then suggested that James forward the e-mail to Jane and that she would follow up to find out if the resources met her quality standards.

Jane was pleasantly surprised to discover how many ILMs already existed on the Battle of Fort Sumter. She also found Pauline's review helpful for quickly narrowing down the list of resources she would consider adding to her course site. She evaluated the best of the ILMs to make sure the content was accurate. She received a follow-up e-mail from Pauline offering to help her integrate any of the ILMs she decided to use into her course website. Jane decided that a brief meeting would be beneficial to make sure the resources were integrated into the LMS so that there would not be any technical problems.

James noticed that more instructors were coming to him interested in supplementing their traditional class resources (i.e., books, journals, and newspapers) with online materials. He decided he would bring up at the next departmental staff and faculty meeting some of the recent requests he had received from faculty and discovered that many of his colleagues were getting similar requests from faculty who were teaching online courses for the university. James talked with his department head and suggested it would be worth partnering with other instructional librarians and the university's Teaching, Learning, and Technology (TLT) Center to support the use and adoption of various types of OERs.

With the blessing of the head of the department, James contacted Pauline and explained his discussion with his colleagues in the libraries and that the library's instruction and user services department was very interested in partnering with TLT to help faculty find and integrate OERs into their courses. Pauline was enthusiastic and explained that many of her colleagues in the TLT had wanted to help raise faculty awareness about the benefits of using OERs to augment their traditional classes and to create more robust and engaging online courses. She explained that she would talk to the director of the TLT and see if a small working group could be formed between some interested librarians and instructional design and technology staff that could lead the collaborative effort to help faculty integrate appropriate OERs into their curricula.

A few days later Pauline received a call from Jane asking her if she could stop by later that day to help her integrate the ILMs into her Civil War course. Pauline explained to Jane the exciting development between the library and the TLT and offered to come to her office later that afternoon. While meeting with Jane, Pauline confirmed with her what she wanted the students to be able to recall after using the ILMs. They agreed that the best ILM to accomplish this was the online simulation of Fort Sumter, which allowed students to choose a historically accurate character and experience firsthand the events that occurred at Fort Sumter in an immersive 3D virtual reality, online environment.

Jane expressed that she liked the Fort Sumter simulation very much but was disappointed that there was no built-in assessment tool with the simulation beyond real-time feedback to the students as they proceeded through the simulation. Pauline pointed out that by embedding the ILM in Moodle a simple quiz could be created that students would need to finish before they got any credit for completing the simulation. Jane liked the idea and worked with Pauline to create a quick low-stakes quiz embedded in her course site that could be completed only after the students played the simulation.

Later that semester, Jane assigned the simulation to her class for the first time. She spent a few moments at the end of a class showing the ILM and explaining what she expected her students to do to complete the assignment before the next class meeting. Prior to the next class, Jane reviewed the results of the quiz her students took after completing the simulation. She was able to contact several students to remind them that they needed to complete the simulation. She was also pleasantly surprised by how well the students scored on the quiz, which had very similar questions to what the students would see on the final test for the course.

During the next class meeting where she would normally lecture on the events that occurred at Fort Sumter, she decided to break the students up into small groups based on the characters they choose and have them discuss what they experienced using the simulation and as a group to come up with a list of the major events that occurred at Fort Sumter. The groups would then briefly present a summary of events at the end of the class. As she walked around the class she noticed that the students were discussing how much they liked using the simulation and seemed excited to share with their classmates the major events that they experienced as the characters in the simulation.

At the end of that same semester, Jane reviewed the final test scores and specifically examined the questions that related to the Battle at Fort Sumter. She was pleased to find that the test scores on those questions were significantly higher when she compared them with several other sections of the course that did not use the ILM over the years. Jane shared her results with her colleagues in the history department and found out that several of them had been asked to teach their courses in hybrid or fully online format and were interested in seeing if they could integrate ILMs into their courses. She offered to contact James and Pauline to have the library and TLT help their department integrate more OERs into their courses.

This story illustrates some of the challenges and opportunities that exist for faculty interested in finding good-quality, interactive learning materials for their courses. While the particulars of the previous story will vary depending on the college or university size and makeup, too often this story cannot happen at many higher educational institutions because faculty, librarians, and instructional designers and technologists are not aware of interactive open educational resources (ILMs), do not know the best sources to search for them, or simply do not have any formal service in place that would make it efficient for faculty to find and integrate ILMs into their courses. As more traditional courses become hybrid (blended) or fully online and have significant components of the course placed online, resources available via the Internet will become increasingly important. Likewise, as technology evolves, as types of interactive resources develop, and as the volume of high-quality ILMs grows, there will be an overabundance of options for faculty from which to choose.

This newly emerging environment will necessitate that faculty, librarians, and other instructional design and technology staff cooperate more closely than ever before. The formation of highly functional, transient teams to assist faculty with the development of hybrid and fully online courses will increasingly be needed to develop high-quality hybrid and online courses (Shank and Bell, 2011; Bass, 2012; Shell, Crawford, and Harris, 2013). The aforementioned story demonstrates this complexity as well as the need to create a formal process and structure to inform faculty and to assist instructors with finding, choosing, and using ILMs in their courses.

The faculty member as instructor and content expert is best suited to judge the quality of the ILMs that they choose to integrate into their courses. However, as the number of sources proliferate to find ILMs, librarians are well positioned to become experts in identifying, providing access to, and searching these databases and repositories. Instructional designers and technologists offer the ability not only to help create and develop new ILMs for their faculty and institutions but also correspondingly to offer valuable thoughts about the best practices in designing hybrid and online courses and to best integrate appropriate ILMs into an instructor's course learning activities and assignments.

The impact this handbook could have may serve as a catalyst for encouraging conversations and facilitating partnerships among instructors, librarians, and educational technologists around the topic of open educational resources, or more specifically a growing subset of OERs: interactive learning materials. By building awareness and providing the first reference guide to the best existing sources to find excellent ILMs and the best practices for searching these sources, this book endeavors to lower the barrier to finding great ILMs. Likewise, this handbook provides good starting points of discussion about how to best to integrate these resources most effectively into college and university courses.

JUST OVER THE HORIZON: A PERSONAL NOTE FROM THE AUTHOR

I have experienced firsthand the impact that appropriate, high-quality ILMs can have on student learning when thoughtfully integrated into a course. As the founding director of the Center for Learning & Teaching at Penn State Berks, I have led teams of faculty in various disciplines, instructional technology staff, librarians, and other faculty development professionals in designing and developing interactive modules and tutorials, games, and simulations for our college's curriculum. Several of these ILM projects appear throughout this book. Our experiences have shown that all of the ILMs the Center for Learning & Teaching has incorporated into courses have positively impacted the faculty and students of those courses.

The instructors who use the ILMs have found that most students enjoy using them. Many faculty have found that they do not need to spend as much time in class as they had in the past explaining the content that the ILMs cover. Additionally, they can tell how much time students spend using the ILMs because they are embedded into the university LMS. We have found that students who make more use the ILMs perform better on course tests and usually have higher GPAs than those who do not.

The student feedback that we received from both the surveys attached to the ILMs and from course evaluations and comment forms demonstrate that students value these resources in their courses. Many students say that the ILMs helped them gain a better understanding of the material beyond what their textbooks or class lectures provided. Also, many students indicated that they enjoyed using the ILMs and that they made learning the material more enjoyable.

As a tenured librarian within Penn State's University Libraries, serving as instructional design librarian for Penn State Berks, I have helped many instructors learn about and find useful ILMs for their courses. I hope that more librarians in the profession would want to learn about ILMs and how useful they could be in their own library or instructional sessions. Likewise, I hope that the academic library profession desires to play a larger role in helping faculty across their institutions learn about, access, and locate valuable ILMs. The opportunities to partner in this endeavor with instructional technology and teaching and learning groups are tremendous.

As an instructor for the communication, arts, and sciences program at Penn State Berks, I have often wanted to integrate resources into my course to help students who are struggling with some aspect of it or who might wish to practice or interact more with the topics we cover. I also like to find resources that can engage and motivate my students to want to learn more. I have found that ILMs can be useful in creating meaningful dialogue, discussions, and inquiry in class, too.

For these reasons and more, I feel strongly that ILMs can be such a useful resource to enhance the learning environment in your course no matter what format it is in: face to face; hybrid or blended; online. Clearly, the trend to offer more online degrees and their related courses will not diminish in the near future. There are too many factors driving the development of these online courses, including the potential cost savings new technologies enable over traditional face-to-face courses; increased access to a larger pool of students; improved flexibility for students who want to take a course on their time to fit into their busy lives; and potentially enhanced learning, retention, and graduation rates for students. All of these trends—combined with the rise of massive open online courses (MOOCs; e.g., Udacity, edX, Coursera) (de Waard et al., 2011), personal learning environments (PLEs) (Attwell, 2007), and the Khan Academy (Thompson, 2011)—signal that higher education is undergoing massive changes.

With this trend, the importance of ILMs will likely increase, but who will support the access and adoption of these resources? My fear is that faculty of higher education, librarians, and educational technologists will not be leading the way. Rather, for-profit publishers and content providers will seize the opportunity to increase their revenues by driving the adoption of ILMs through their textbooks and related digital content. If this happens, educators could become marginalized and not have as much say in what the future of ILMs looks like. The cost of these resources will likely increase. It is possible that an open market for the resources will develop similar to the iTunes App Store where students can buy an educational app for only a few dollars. However, it is still too early to predict how and when this might happen.

Also, there is a danger that these resources will become considered good enough to replace the face-to-face time that currently exists in higher education. I strongly feel that computers and their related tools like ILMs can be used to enhance instruction but should never be used to completely replace personal connection formed through in-person instruction. The human-to-human connection is simply too important to be completely replaced by computer-mediated communication.

I believe that the best use of ILMs is to enhance the interaction students have with course material, their peers, and their instructors. These resources can be power tools to motivate and remediate student learning. They also allow the instructor to move away from the model of sage on the stage to the guide by their side. If high-quality ILMs become the norm and can be widely adopted by faculty as part of their course resources, colleges and universities will be able to transform the learning environment, no matter what form it takes for their students, and to help to improve student learning, achieving greater student retention and graduation rates.

REFERENCES

Ainsworth, S. "Deft a Conceptual Framework for Considering Learning with Multiple Representations." *Learning and Instruction*, 2006, 16(3), 183–198.

Aldrich, C. *Learning Online with Games, Simulations, and Virtual Worlds: Strategies for Online Instruction* (Vol. 11). San Francisco, CA: Jossey-Bass, 2009.

Alessi, Stephen M., and Trollip, S. R. *Computer-Based Instruction: Methods and Development.* Englewood Cliffs, NJ: Prentice Hall, 1991.

Amaral, K. E., and Shank, J. D. "Enhancing Student Learning and Retention with Blended Learning Class Guides." *Educause Quarterly*, 2010, 33(4). http://www.educause.edu/EDUCAUSE+Quarterly/EDUCAUSEQuarterlyMagazineVolum/EnhancingStudentLearningandRet/219137.

Anderson, L. W. *A Taxonomy for Learning, Teaching, and Assessing: A Revision of Bloom's Taxonomy of Educational Objectives.* New York: Longman, 2009.

Angelo, T. A., and Cross, K. P. *Classroom Assessment Techniques: A Handbook for College Teachers.* San Francisco, CA: Jossey-Bass, 1993.

Association of College and Research Libraries. "Peer-Reviewed Instructional Materials Online Database (PRIMO)." July 2012. http://www.ala.org/CFApps/Primo/public/search.cfm.

Atkins, D. E., Brown, J. S., and Hammond, A. L. *A Review of the Open Educational Resources (OER) Movement Achievements, Challenges, and New Opportunities.* San Francisco, CA: Creative Common, 2007. http://www.hewlett.org/uploads/files/ReviewoftheOERMovement.pdf.

Attwell, G. "Personal Learning Environments—The Future of eLearning?" *eLearning Papers*, 2007, 2(1), 1–7.

August, R. J., Lopez, G. W., Yokomoto, C. F., and Buchanan, W. W. "*Heuristic Beliefs about Problem Solving in Technology Courses and Their Impact on Success on Problem Solving Exams.*" Proceedings from the Frontiers in Education Conference, Boston, MA, November 2002.

Barkley, E. F. *Student Engagement Techniques: A Handbook for College Faculty*. San Francisco, CA: Jossey-Bass, 2010.

Barr, R. B., and Tagg, J. "From Teaching to Learning— A New Paradigm for Undergraduate Education." *Change: The Magazine of Higher Learning*, 1995, 27(6), 12–26.

Bass, R. "Disrupting Ourselves: The Problem of Learning in Higher Education." *EDUCAUSE Review*, 2012, 47(2). http://www.educause.edu/ero/article/disrupting-ourselves-problem-learning-higher-education.

Bean, J. C. *Engaging Ideas: The Professor's Guide to Integrating Writing, Critical Thinking, and Active Learning in the Classroom*. San Francisco, CA: Jossey-Bass, 2011.

Bellinger, G., Castro, D., and Mills, A. "Data, Information, Knowledge, and Wisdom." *The Way of Systems*. 2004. http://www.systems-thinking.org/dikw/dikw.htm.

Blackboard Inc. "Blackboard and McGraw-Hill Partner to Integrate McGraw-Hill Digital Content & Tools into Blackboard's Learning Management Systems." Press release. July 14, 2010. http://www.prnewswire.com/news-releases/blackboard-and-mcgraw-hill-partner-to-integrate-mcgraw-hill-digital-content—tools-into-blackboards-learning-management-systems-98445079.html.

Block, J. H. "Mastery Learning: The Current State of the Craft." *Educational Leadership*, 1979, 37(2), 114–117.

Briggs, L. J., Gustafson, K. L., and Tillman, M. *Instructional Design: Principles and Applications* (2d ed.). Englewood Cliffs, NJ: Educational Technology Publications, 1991.

Burton J. K., and Merrill, P. F. "Needs Assessment: Goals, Needs, and Priorities." In L. J. Briggs (ed.), *Instructional Design: Principles and Applications*. Englewood Cliffs, NJ: Educational Technology Publications, 1991, p. 21.

Cengage Learning. "Learning Unleashed: Cengage Learning 'Taps' into Minds of Students with MindTap™, First-of-Its-Kind Personal Learning Experience." March 2011. http://www.prnewswire.com/news-releases/learning-unleashed-cengage-learning-taps-into-minds-of-students-with-mindtap-first-of-its-kind-personal-learning-experience-117232893.html.

Chickering, A., and Gamson, Z. "Seven Principles for Good Practice in Undergraduate Education." *AAHE Bulletin*. March 1987. http://www.eric.ed.gov/ERICWebPortal/search/detailmini.jsp?_nfpb=true&_&ERICExtSearch_SearchValue_0=ED282491&ERICExtSearch_SearchType_0=no&accno=ED282491.

Chickering, A. W., and Ehrmann, S. C. "Implementing the Seven Principles: Technology as Lever." *AAHE Bulletin*, 1996, 49(2), 3–6.

Chickering, A. W., Gamson, Z. F., and Susan, J. P. *Seven Principles for Good Practice in Undergraduate Education*. Racine, WI: Johnson Foundation, 1987.

Churchill, D. "Towards a Useful Classification of Learning Objects." *Educational Technology Research and Development*, 2007, 55(5), 479–497.

Claxton, C. S., and Ralston, Y. *Learning Styles: Their Impact on Teaching and Administration*. Washington, DC: American Association for Higher Education, 1978.

Conrad, R. M., and Donaldson, J. A. *Engaging the Online Learner: Activities and Resources for Creative Instruction* (Vol. 36). San Francisco, CA: Jossey-Bass, 2011.

Creswell, J. *Educational Research: Planning, Conducting, and Evaluating Quantitative and Qualitative Research.* Upper Saddle River, NJ: Prentice Hall, 2002.

de Waard, I., Abajian, S., Gallagher, M. S., Hogue, R., Keskin, N., Koutropoulos, A., and Rodriguez, O. C. "Using mLearning and MOOCs to Understand Chaos, Emergence, and Complexity in Education." *International Review of Research in Open and Distance Learning*, 2011, 12(7), 94–115.

Deubel, P. "An Investigation of Behaviorist and Cognitive Approaches to Instructional Multimedia Design." *Journal of Educational Multimedia and Hypermedia*, 2003, 12(1), 63–90.

Dickey, M. D. "Engaging by Design: How Engagement Strategies in Popular Computer and Video Games Can Inform Instructional Design." *Educational Technology Research and Development*, 2005, 53(2), 67–83.

Dimitrov, D. M., and Rumrill Jr., P. D. "Pretest–Posttest Designs and Measurement of Change." *Work*, 2003, 20(2), 159–165.

Durka, G. *The Teacher's Calling: A Spirituality for Those Who Teach.* New York: Paulist Press, 2002.

EDUCAUSE. "7 Things You Should Know about Flipped Classrooms." *Things You Should Know About … * February 2012. http://net.educause.edu/ir/library/pdf/ELI7081.pdf.

Gagné, R. M. *The Conditions of Learning and Theory of Instruction.* New York: Holt, Rinehart and Winston, 1985.

Gagné, R. M., Wager, W. W., Golas, K. C., and Keller, J. M. *Principles of Instructional Design.* Belmont, CA: Wadsworth, 2005.

Garrison, D. R., and Norman, D. V. *Blended Learning in Higher Education: Framework, Principles, and Guidelines.* San Francisco, CA: Jossey-Bass, 2008.

Handal, B., and Herrington, A. "Re-examining Categories of Computer-Based Learning in Mathematics Education." *Contemporary Issues in Technology and Teacher Education*, 2003, 3(3), 275–287.

Hargittai, E. "Digital Na(t)ives? Variation in Internet Skills and Uses among Members of the 'Net Generation.'" *Sociological Inquiry*, 2010, 80(1), 92–113.

Harlen, W., and James, M. "Assessment and Learning: Differences and Relationships between Formative and Summative Assessment." *Assessment in Education: Principles, Policy & Practice*, 1997, 4(3), 365–379.

Heer, R. "A Model of Learning Objectives." Iowa State University, Center for Excellence in Learning and Teaching. January 2012. http://www.celt.iastate.edu/teaching/Revised Blooms1.html.

Helsper, E. J., and Eynon, R. "Digital Natives: Where Is the Evidence?" *British Educational Research Journal*, 2010, 36(3), 503–520.

Hubing, N., Oglesby, D., Philpot, T., Yellamraju, V., Hall, R., and Flori, R. "Interactive Learning Tools: Animating Statics." Paper presented at the American Society for Engineering Education Annual Conference, Montreal, Canada, June 2002.

Johnson, B., and Christensen, L. *Educational Research: Quantitative, Qualitative, and Mixed Approaches* (3d ed.). Thousand Oaks, CA: SAGE, 2008.

Johnson, L., Smith, R., Willis, H., Levine, A., and Haywood, K. "The 2011 Horizon Report." Austin, TX: New Media Consortium, 2011. http://net.educause.edu/ir/library/pdf/HR2011.pdf

Johnstone, S. M. "Open Educational Resources Serve the World." *EDUCAUSE Quarterly*, 2005, 8(3), 15–18.

Jones, C., Ramanau, R., Cross, S., and Healing, G. "Net Generation or Digital Natives: Is There a Distinct New Generation Entering University?" *Computers and Education*, 2010, 54(3), 722–732.

Kaw, A., Collier, N., Keteltas, M., Paul, J., and Besterfield, G. "Holistic but Customized Resources for a Course in Numerical Methods." *Computer Applications in Engineering Education*, 2003, 11, 203–210.

Kirkpatrick, D. I. *Evaluating Training Programs* (2d ed.). San Francisco, CA: Berrett-Koehler, 1998.

Kolb, A. Y., and Kolb, D. A. "Learning Styles and Learning Spaces: Enhancing Experiential Learning in Higher Education." *Academy of Management Learning & Education*, 2005, 4(2), 193–212.

Krathwohl, D. R. "A Revision of Bloom's Taxonomy: An Overview." *Theory into Practice*, 2002, 41(4), 212–218.

Lane, J. L., and Cawley, J. M. (2001). "Issue Reaction: Inquiry-Based Learning in the College Classroom." Innovations in Undergraduate Research and Honors Education: Proceedings of the Second Schreyer National Conference. Paper 21. 2001. http://digitalcommons.unl.edu/cgi/viewcontent.cgi?article=1020&context=nchcschreyer2.

McMartin, F. "MERLOT: A Model for User Involvement in Digital Library Design and Implementation." *Journal of Digital Information*, 2006, 5(3).

Meyers, C., and Thomas, B. J. *Promoting Active Learning: Strategies for the College Classroom*. San Francisco, CA: Jossey-Bass, 1993.

Mirizzi, R., Ragone, A., Noia, T. D., and Sciascio, E. D. "Semantic Wonder Cloud: Exploratory Search in Dbpedia." *Lecture Notes in Computer Science (including Subseries Lecture Notes in Artificial Intelligence and Lecture Notes in Bioinformatics)*, 2010, 138–149.

Moseley, J. L., and Heaney, M. J. "Needs Assessment across Disciplines." *Performance Improvement Quarterly*, 1994, 7(1), 60–79.

Novak, M. "Learning in 1999 A.D. (1967)." *Paleofuture*. January 31, 2008. http://www.paleofuture.com/blog/2008/1/31/learning-in-1999-ad-1967.html.

Oblinger, D., and Oblinger, J. L. *Educating the Net Generation*. Boulder, CO: EDUCAUSE, 2005.

Orme, W. A. "A Study of the Residual Impact of the Texas Information Literacy Tutorial on the Information-Seeking Ability of First Year College Students." *College and Research Libraries*, 2004, 65(3), 205–215.

Pearson. "EQUELLA 5.1 Digital Repository." October 18, 2011. http://www.prnewswire.com/news-releases/pearson-releases-equella-51-digital-repository-132060873.html.

Penn State. "Penn State MTO Repository." May 2011. http://tlt.its.psu.edu/mto/index.html.

Penn State Berks. "Math 110 eLearning Project." January 2012. http://www.bk.psu.edu/StudentServices/IT/math.htm.

Picciano, A. "Blending with Purpose: The Multimodal Model." *Journal of the Research Center for Educational Technology*, 2009, 5(1), 4–14.

Pickard, M. J. "The New Bloom's Taxonomy: An Overview for Family and Consumer Sciences." *Journal of Family and Consumer Sciences Education*, 2007, 25(1), 45–55.

Powers, S., and Guan, S. "Examining the Range of Student Needs in the Design and Development of a Web-Based Course." *Instructional and Cognitive Impacts of Web-Based Education*, 2000, 200–216.

Prensky, M. "Digital Natives, Digital Immigrants Part 2: Do They Really Think Differently?" *On the Horizon*, 2001, 9(6), 1–6.

Prensky, M. *Teaching Digital Natives: Partnering for Real Learning*. Thousand Oaks, CA: Corwin, 2010.

Rieber, L. P. "Seriously Considering Play: Designing Interactive Learning Environments Based on the Blending of Microworlds, Simulations, and Games." *Educational Technology Research & Development*, 1996, 44(2), 43–58.

Riffel, S., and Sibley, D. "Using Web-Based Instruction to Improve Large Undergraduate Biology Courses: An Evaluation of a Hybrid Course Format." *Computers and Education*, 2004, 44(3), 217–235.

Schuh, K. L., and Barab, S. A. "Philosophical Perspectives." In J. M. Spector, M. D. Merrill, J. van errionboer, and M. P. Driscoll (eds.), *Handbook of Research on Educational Communications and Technology*. New York: Lawrence Erlbaum Associates. 2008, pp. 213–264.

Shank, J. "The Emergence of Learning Objects: the Reference Librarian's Role." *Research Strategies*, 2003, 19(3–4), 193–203.

Shank, J. D., and Bell, S. "Blended Librarianship." *Reference & User Services Quarterly*, 2011, 51(2), 105–110.

Shell, L., Crawford, S., and Harris, P. "Aided and Embedded: The Team Approach to Instructional Design." *Journal of Library & Information Services in Distance Learning*, 2013, 7(1–2), 143–155.

Slavin, R. E. *Student Team Learning: A Practical Guide to Cooperative Learning*. Washington, DC: NEA Professional Library, National Education Association, 1991.

Thompson, C. "How Khan Academy Is Changing the Rules of Education." *Wired Magazine*, 2011, 1 5.

U.S. Department of Education, Office of Planning, Evaluation and Policy Development, Policy and Program Studies. *Evaluation of Evidence-Based Practices in Online*

Learning: A Meta-Analysis and Review of Online Learning Studies. 2010. Washington, DC. http://www2.ed.gov/rschstat/eval/tech/evidence-based-practices/finalreport.pdf.

Walvoord, B. E., and Pool, K. J. "Enhancing Pedagogical Productivity." *New Directions for Higher Education*, 1998, (103), 35–48.

Walvoord, B.E.F., and Anderson, V. J. *Effective Grading: A Tool for Learning and Assessment in College.* San Francisco, CA: Jossey-Bass, 2010.

INDEX

A

Active learning, 137

ADDIE. *See* Analyze, Design, Development, Implement, and Evaluate

Adobe Flash, 27, 123

Advanced search techniques, 26; in JORUM, 58–59; in MERLOT, 43–44; in NCLOR, 70; with NSDL, 108; in OER Commons, 50

Agenda approach, 131

American Association of Museums, 100

Analyze, Design, Development, Implement, and Evaluate (ADDIE), 5

App Store, 93

Apple, 93; QuickTime, 27

Apps, 93

ARIADNE: browsing with, 53; description of, 51–52; evaluation of, 54–55; features of, 52; quality, usability, currency, and reliability of, 52; searchability of, 53; searching with, 53–54

Assessment, 143–144; categories, 117; checklist, 116; course needs, 115–116; of digital learning materials, 114–117; formative, 150–151; with in-class quizzes, 146; of learners, 115–117;

with LMSs, 145; with mastery learning, 145–146; in math 110 case study, 147–153; performance, 6, 7, 139; with pretest and posttest, 144–145; with scientific method, 147; summative, 151–153

Attention span, 5

Audience, 28

Australia, 60

B

Battle at Fort Sumter, 156, 158

Berks College case study, 147–153

Bloom's revised taxonomy, 117–118

Browsing, 23–24; with ARIADNE, 53; entertainment media companies, 88–91; with JORUM, 57–58; with KLD, 73–74; with MERLOT, 42; with NCLOR, 68–69; with NSDL, 106–107; with OER Commons, 48–49; with PRIMO, 102; with Wisc-Online, 65

Built-in feedback, 122–123, 137–138

C

Calculus learning modules, 149–150

Canada, 60

Cengage Learning's Higher Education division, 87

Change: climate, 94; in higher education, xi; from technology, 155

Class guide, 131

Classroom: activities, 134; flip, 132–133

Climate change, 94

Cognitive process, 118

Colleges and universities: courses and courseware initiatives, 79–80; emerging tools and search trends in, 79–80; flowchart for searching on sites of, 77; Harvard Medical School, 78; ILM searches through, 76–79; ILMs by, 30, 61–80; Iowa State University, 120; KLD, 71–75; NCLOR, 67–71; nonprofit educational repositories and libraries, 62–63; Pennsylvania State University, 76, 78, 124–126; University of Colorado at Boulder, 78–79; Web search tools, 78–79; Wisc-Online, 63–66. See also Higher education

Constructive innovation, xi–xii

Content quality, 120

Contextual Targeting Tool, 22

Course needs assessment, 115–116

Course websites, 156–157

Courses: MOOCs, 79, 84

Courseware initiatives, 79–80

Creation information search tool, 103–104

Currency: of ARIADNE, 52; DLM, 28; of JORUM, 56; of KLD, 72; of MERLOT, 41; of NCLOR, 68; of NSDL, 105; OER Commons, 48; of Wisc-Online, 64

D

Data objects, 12–13

Dates, 28

DC. See Discovery Channel

DE. See Discover Education

Digital components, 14

Digital learning materials: assessment of, 114–117; evaluation criteria for, 119–124; learning activities, 117–119

Digital libraries, 29; future of, 59–60; NSDL, 104–109

Digital revolution, 11–12

Digitization, 4

Discover Education (DE), 91

Discovery Channel (DC), 88–89, 91; searching with, 92

Disruptive innovation, xi–xii

ILM currency, 28

E

Educational software companies: ILMs by, 92–94; searching with, 93–94; video list for, 84

EDUCAUSE, 86, 101

Energy, 94

Energyville, 94

Entertainment media companies: browsing, 88–91; DC, 88–89, 91, 92; ILMs by, 30, 87–92; interacting with, 4; PBS, 89–91; programming by, 87–88; searching with, 92; technological devices relating to, 87–88; video list for, 84

Europe, 51–55

Evaluation: of ARIADNE, 54–55; of JORUM, 59; of KLD, 75; of MERLOT, 44–45; of NCLOR, 70–71; of NSDL, 108–109; of OER Commons, 50–51; of Wisc-Online, 66

Evaluation criteria: for built-in feedback, 122–123; content quality, 120; for digital learning materials, 119–124; for interactivity, 122; at Iowa State University, 120; of learning activity types, 120–122; six-step decision tree, 121; technical check, 123–124; for usability, 123

Expectations, high, 139–140

F

Face-to-face interactions, 162

Faculty. *See* Teachers

Feedback: built-in, 122–123, 137–138; from learners, 6; prompt, 137–138; by students, 160

First exposure, 132–133

Folder link approach, 131

Formative assessment, 150–151

Formats, 27; media, 50

Fort Sumter simulation, 158

Funding, 60

G

Gagne's Nine Events of Instruction, 5–7, 8

Games: "games learning OR higher education" Google search, 139; learning, 8; online, 17, 119

Good learning modules, 8

Good practice principles, 134–135

Google: Contextual Targeting Tool by, 22; "games learning OR higher education" search, 139; searching with, 76, 79, 139

Governmental organizations: ILMs by, 104–110; NASA, 109–110; NSDL, 104–109; video list for searching, 96

Guidance, 6

H

Harvard Medical School, 78

Hierarchy, 12–14

High expectations, 139–140

Higher education: Cengage Learning's Higher Education division, 87; change in, xi; emerging trends and search tools in, 79–80; "games learning OR higher education" Google search, 139; instructional transformation in,

xii–xiii; McGraw-Hill's Higher Education division, 86; Pearson's Higher Education division, 86; Wiley's Higher Education division, 87

I

ILMs. *See* Interactive learning materials

Implementation process: class guide or agenda approach, 131; folder link approach, 131; for ILMs, 129–140; instructional approaches, 132–140; lessons or modules link approach, 131–132; syllabus approach, 130–131

In-class quizzes, 146

Information: creation information search tool, 103–104; hierarchy, 12–14; objects, 12–13; scientists, 12; TILT, 27

Innovation, xi–xii

Instructional approaches: active learning, 137; first exposure and classroom flip, 132–133; good practice principles, 134–135; high expectations, 139–140; learning remediation, 133–134; learning styles and strengths relating to, 140; matrix, 133; prompt feedback, 137–138; student cooperation, 136; student-faculty contact, 135–136; time on task, 138–139

Instructional challenges, 148–149

Instructional transformation, xii–xiii

Interaction types, 31

Interactive learning materials (ILMs): ADDIE relating to, 5; aspects of, 5–7; audience, 28; best uses for, 162; browsing collections, 23–24; built-in feedback, 122–123, 137–138; as classroom activities, 134; by colleges and universities, 30, 61–80; content quality, 120; defining, 12, 15; digital components of, 14; DLM currency, 28; by educational software companies, 92–94; by entertainment media companies, 30,

Interactive learning materials (ILMs): *(continued)*
87–92; in Europe, 51–55; formats, 27; by governmental organizations, 104–110; implementation process, 129–140; importance of, 161; interface design, 31–32; key elements of, 15–16; language, 28; learners' attention to, 5; learning continuum with, 8; learning objects of, 12–13; LMSs and, 130; major components of, 4–5; as multimedia, 14; by museums, 30, 97–100; new paradigm with, xiii–xvi; in North America, 36–51; objectives of, 5; potential of, xiv–xv; by professional organizations, 101–104; quality of, 31; rise of, 4–7; search steps for locating, 21–23, 28–30, 62, 76–79; search taxonomy, 22, 28–30, 36; searching collections, 24–26; selection process, 111–126; by software companies, 30; student feedback on, 160; subject and keyword identification, 22–23; technical check, 123–124; terminology referring to, 30; by textbook publishers, 84–87; type identification, 26–27; in United Kingdom, 55–59; usability, 123

Interactivity, 122
Interface design, 31–32
Iowa State University, 120
iTunes, 93

J

JORUM: advanced search technique in, 58–59; browsing, 57–58; description of, 55–56; evaluation of, 59; features of, 56; quality, usability, currency, and reliability of, 56–57; searchability of, 57; searching with, 58–59

K

Kentucky Learning Depot (KLD): browsing with, 73–74; description of, 71–72; evaluation of, 75; features of, 72; quality, usability, currency, and reliability of, 72; searchability of, 72–73; searching with, 74
Keywords: identification, 22–23; in MERLOT, 43, 44; in Wisc-Online, 65
KLD. *See* Kentucky Learning Depot
Knowledge: objects, 12–13; prior, 6; retention of, 7

L

Language, 28
Learners: assessment of, 115–117; attention of, to ILMs, 5; feedback from, 6; guidance for, 6; knowledge retention, 7; performance of, 6, 7; prior knowledge of, 6; stimulating, 6; student cooperation, 136; student feedback, 160; student-faculty contact, 135–136
Learning: active, 137; analytics, 138–139; continuum, 8; digital materials for, 114–124; games, 8; mastery, 145–146; objects, 12–13; remediation, 133–134; styles and strengths, 140. *See also* Assessment
Learning activities: Bloom's revised taxonomy, 117–118; cognitive process, 118; digital learning materials, 117–119; evaluation criteria of, 120–122; with learning modules, 119
Learning management systems (LMSs), 84, 85–86; assessment with, 145; ILMs and, 130
Learning modules: calculus, 149–150; defining, 16; good, 8; learning activities with, 119; linear sequence in, 16; online games, 17, 119; online

simulations, 17, 119; tutorials, 16–17, 27, 40–41, 44, 119

Learning Object Repository Network (LORN), 60

Lessons approach, 131–132

Libraries: for colleges and universities, 62–63; digital, 29, 59–60; nonprofit online, 39, 62–63; NSDL, 104–109; technology relating to, xiii

Linear sequence, 16

LMSs. *See* Learning management systems

LORN. *See* Learning Object Repository Network

M

Massive online open courses (MOOCs), 79, 84

Mastery learning, 145–146

Material type, 50

Math 110 case study: assessment in, 147–153; calculus learning modules in, 149–150; formative assessment in, 150–151; instructional challenges in, 148–149; summative assessment in, 151–153

McGraw-Hill's Higher Education division, 86

Media format, 50

MERLOT. *See* Multimedia Educational Resource for Learning and Online Teaching

Microsoft PowerPoint, 27

Mobile devices, 93

Modules link approach, 131–132

MOOCs. *See* Massive online open courses

Multimedia: ILMs as, 14; in tutorials, 17

Multimedia Educational Resource for Learning and Online Teaching (MERLOT), 24–26, 29; advanced search techniques with, 43–44; background on, 36–38; browsing, 42; evaluation of, 44–45; evolution of, 38; features of, 38–39, 40; keyword search, 43, 44; quality, usability, currency, and reliability, 39–41; searchability, 42; searching with, 42–44; strengths and weaknesses, 41; "Team Dynamics and Building" tutorial, 44; tutorials, 40–41, 44

Museum of Natural History, 100

Museums: American Association of Museums, 100; ILMs by, 30, 97–100; Smithsonian, 97–100; video list for searching, 96

N

National Aeronautics and Space Administration (NASA), 109–110

National Science Digital Library (NSDL): advanced search techniques with, 108; browsing with, 106–107; description of, 104; evaluation of, 108–109; features of, 104–105; quality, usability, currency, and reliability of, 105; searchability of, 105–106; searching with, 107–108

NCLOR. *See* North Carolina Learning Object Repository

Net Generation, 1

1999 A.D., xii

Nonprofit online educational repositories and libraries, 39, 62–63

North America: ILMs in, 36–51; MERLOT, 24–26, 29, 36–45; OER Commons, 46–51

North Carolina Learning Object Repository (NCLOR): advanced search techniques in, 70; browsing with, 68–69; description of, 67; evaluation of, 70–71; features of, 67; quality, usability, currency, and reliability of, 68; searchability of, 68; searching with, 69–70

NSDL. *See* National Science Digital Library

O

OER Commons. *See* Open Educational Resources Commons
OERs. *See* Open educational resources
Online courses, 159; MOOCs, 84
Online games, 17, 119
Online simulations, 119; defining, 17; web-based, 17
Open educational resources (OERs): course websites integrated with, 156–157; future of, 59–60; ILM learning continuum, 8; traditional resources compared to, xiii
Open Educational Resources Commons (OER Commons): advanced search with, 50; browsing, 48–49; description of, 46; evaluation of, 50–51; features of, 46; material type and media format in, 50; quality, usability, currency, and reliability of, 47–48; searchability, 48; searching with, 49–50
Openclass, 86

P

PBS. *See* Public Broadcasting Network
Pearson's Higher Education division, 86
Peer-Reviewed Instructional Materials Online (PRIMO), 30; browsing with, 102; collections, 101; creation information search tool, 103–104; description of, 101; searchability of, 101–102; searching with, 102–104
Pennsylvania State University, 76, 78, 124–126; Berks College, 147–153
Performance: of learners, 6, 7; tracking functions, 139. *See also* Assessment
Personal connections, 162

Personalized learning environment (PLE), 85
Posttests, 144–145
PowerPoint, 27
Pretests, 144–145
PRIMO. *See* Peer-Reviewed Instructional Materials Online
Prior knowledge, 6
Professional organizations: ILMs by, 101–104; video list for searching, 96
Programming, 87–88
Prompt feedback, 137–138
Public Broadcasting Network (PBS), 89–90; teachers, 90–91

Q

Quality: of ARIADNE, 52; content, 120; ILM, 31; of JORUM, 56–57; of KLD, 72; MERLOT, 39–41; of NCLOR, 68; of NSDL, 105; OER Commons, 47–48; of Wisc-Online, 63–64
Quick Start Guide, 36, 37–38
QuickTime, 27
Quizzes, 146

R

Reliability: of ARIADNE, 52; of JORUM, 56; of KLD, 72; MERLOT, 39–41; of NCLOR, 68; of NSDL, 105; OER Commons, 48; of Wisc-Online, 64
Repositories, 29; for colleges and universities, 62–63; LORN, 60; nonprofit online, 39, 62–63; Quick Start Guide for, 36, 37–38. *See also specific repositories*
Resources: OERs, xiii, 8, 59–60, 156–157; STEM, 105; technology relating to, 4; traditional, xiii, 4, 57. *See also specific resources*
Retention, 7

Robert Gagne's Nine Events of Instruction, 5–7, 8

S

Scientific method, 147

Scientists, 12

Search taxonomy, 22, 28–30, 36

Searchability: of ARIADNE, 53; of JORUM, 57; of KLD, 72–73; MERLOT, 42; NCLOR, 68; NSDL, 105–106; OER Commons, 48; PRIMO, 101–102; Wisc-Online, 64–65

Searching: with American Association of Museums, 100; with ARIADNE, 53–54; collections, 24–26; for college and university nonprofit educational repositories and libraries, 62–63; creation information search tool, 103–104; with DC, 92; with educational software companies, 93–94; emerging search tools, 79–80; with entertainment media companies, 92; flowchart, of college and university sites, 77; with Google, 76, 79, 139; with JORUM, 58–59; with KLD, 74; locating ILMs, 21–23, 28–30, 62, 76–79; with MERLOT, 42–44; for museums, professional organizations, and governmental organizations, 96; with NASA, 109–110; with NCLOR, 69–70; for nonprofit online educational repositories and libraries, 39; with NSDL, 107–108; with OER Commons, 49–50; with PRIMO, 102–104; with SI, 97; with Smithsonian Collections Search Center, 98; with Smithsonian Education site, 98–100; with social media, 80; techniques, 24–25; for textbook publishers, entertainment media, and educational software companies, 84; video list for, 39, 62–63, 84, 96; Web

tools for, 78–79; with Wisc-Online, 65–66. *See also* Advanced search techniques

Selection process: case study, 124–126; digital learning material assessment, 114–117; digital learning material evaluation criteria, 119–124; digital learning material learning activities, 117–119; for ILMs, 111–126; stages of, 114

Seven Principles for Good Practice, 135

SI. *See* Smithsonian Institution

Six-step decision tree, 121

Smithsonian Collections Search Center, 98

Smithsonian Education site, 98–100

Smithsonian Institution (SI), 97

Smithsonian Museums, 97–100

Social media, 80

Software companies: educational, 84, 92–94; ILMs by, 30

STEM digital resources, 105

Stimulating learners, 6

Students: cooperation of, 136; faculty contact with, 135–136; feedback from, 160. *See also* Learners

Subject identification, 22–23

Summative assessment, 151–153

Summative test, 146

Syllabus approach, 130–131

T

Teachers: faculty assistance, 159; PBS, 90–91; student-faculty contact, 135–136

"Team Dynamics and Building" tutorial, 44

Technical check, 123–124

Technological devices: entertainment media companies relating to, 87–88; mobile devices, 93

Technology: change from, 155; digital revolution, 11–12; libraries relating to, xiii; resources relating to, 4

Texas Information Literacy Tutorial (TILT), 27

Textbook publishers: Cengage Learning's Higher Education division, 87; ILMs by, 84–87; McGraw-Hill's Higher Education division, 86; Openclass, 86; Pearson's Higher Education division, 86; video list for, 84; Wiley's Higher Education division, 87

Textbooks, 13

TILT. *See* Texas Information Literacy Tutorial

Time on task, 138–139

Timeliness, 28

Tracking functions, 139

Traditional resources: digitization of, 4; OERs compared to, xiii; supplementing, 57

Tutorials, 119; MERLOT, 40–41, 44; multimedia in, 17; structure of, 16–17; "Team Dynamics and Building," 44; TILT, 27. *See also* Learning modules

Type identification, 26–27

U

United Kingdom, 55–59

Universities. *See* Colleges and universities

University of Colorado at Boulder, 78–79

Usability: of ARIADNE, 52; evaluation criteria for, 123; of ILMs, 123; of JORUM, 56–57; of KLD, 72; MERLOT, 39–41; of NCLOR, 68; of NSDL, 105; OER Commons, 47–48; of Wisc-Online, 63–64

V

Valery, Paul, xii

Video list: for college and university non-profit educational repositories and libraries, 62–63; for museums, professional organizations, and governmental organizations, 96; for searching nonprofit online educational repositories and libraries, 39; for textbook publishers, entertainment media, and educational software companies, 84

W

Web search tools, 78–79

Web-based online simulations, 17

Websites, course, 156–157

Wiley's Higher Education division, 87

Wisc-Online: browsing, 65; description of, 63; evaluation of, 66; features of, 63, 64; keyword search with, 65; quality, usability, currency, and reliability of, 63–64; searchability, 64–65; searching with, 65–66

Wisconsin Online, 29